PENGUIN BOOKS

UNPLUGGING THE PLUG-IN DRUG

Marie Winn has written twelve books both children, the most recent being *Children With* Revised Edition of *The Plug-In Drug,* both guin. She is a contributor to *The New York Times Magazine* and the mother of two sons. The family owns one television set, which is used on special occasions.

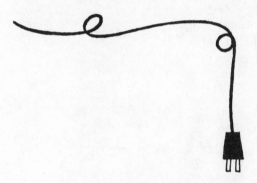

Also by Marie Winn

FOR ADULTS

The Playgroup Book (*with Mary A. Porcher*)
The Baby Reader
Children Without Childhood
The Plug-In Drug (two editions)

FOR CHILDREN

The Fireside Book of Children's Songs
The Fireside Book of Fun & Game Songs
The Fisherman Who Needed a Knife
The Man Who Made Fine Tops
Shiver, Gobble & Snore
"The Sick Book"
The Thief Catcher
What Shall We Do & Allee Galloo

· MARIE WINN ·

Unplugging
the Plug-In Drug

DRAWINGS BY KARLA KUSKIN

PENGUIN BOOKS

To the No-TV Week kids at P.S. 84 and P.S. 166, whose will and determination to meet this challenge of a TV Turn-Off inspired me to start this book, and

To two remarkable teachers—Robin Shephard and Esther Forrest, whose interest and enthusiasm gave me courage to finish it.

PENGUIN BOOKS
Viking Penguin Inc., 40 West 23rd Street,
New York, New York 10010, U.S.A.
Penguin Books Ltd, 27 Wrights Lane, London W8 5TZ (Publishing & Editorial)
and Harmondsworth, Middlesex,
England (Distribution & Warehouse)
Penguin Books Australia Ltd, Ringwood, Victoria, Australia
Penguin Books Canada Limited, 2801 John Street, Markham, Ontario, Canada L3R 1B4
Penguin Books (N.Z.) Ltd, 182–190 Wairau Road, Auckland 10, New Zealand

First published in simultaneous hardcover and paperback editions by Viking Penguin Inc. 1987
Published simultaneously in Canada

Author's note: The names of the families described in the case histories have been changed to protect their privacy. Their stories, however, and all other names in this book, are real.

Grateful acknowledgment is made for permission to reprint the following copyrighted material:
"Family Circus" and "Hi & Lois" cartoons. By permission of King Features Syndicate Division.
"Nancy" cartoon. © 1984 United Features Syndicate, Inc.
Essay by Joseph A. Feather originally in the Society for the Eradication of Television (SET) Newsletter, July 1986. By permission of the author.
"Out the Window? Second Thoughts on TV" by Dottie Lamm originally in The Denver Post, February 23, 1986. By permission of the author.

LIBRARY OF CONGRESS CATALOGING IN PUBLICATION DATA
Winn, Marie.
Unplugging the plug-in drug.
Includes index.
1. Television audiences. 2. Television
programs. 3. Television broadcasting. I. Title.
HE8700.65.W56 1987   302.2'345   86-30655
ISBN 0-14-008895-4

Printed in the United States of America
R. R. Donnelley & Sons Company, Harrisonburg, Virginia
Set in Sabon
Designed by Victoria Hartman

Acknowledgments

Special thanks to:

Nancy DeSalvo, Robin Del Giudice, Esther Forrest, Sarah Kahn, Tanya Kauffman, Sandy Mann, Mike Miller, Steve Miller, Sarah Paul, Sandy Pezzino, Nancy Pike, Robin Shephard, Peggy Steinfels, Martha Thornton.

Staff and parents at P.S. 84:

Sid Morison, Irma Figueroa, Graciela Flemister, Esther Forrest, Mary Forsyth, Irene Kazepis, Julia Matlaw, Leonore Pando, Robin Shephard, Victoria Wilson, Lorraine Cohen, Julie Cadenhead, Ann Cook-Mack, Sonya Cranston, Jordan Davidson, Eva Goenaga, Barbara Iverson, David Kalke, Susan Ship, Karen Wilson, Randye Winfield.

And finally the kids:

Nzinga Adelona, Michelle Amaro, Onel Batista, Julie Berrios, Belinda Brooks, David Brown, Ivy Colomba, Joseph Diaz, Jonathan Falk, Silvia Heredia, Maria Heres, Lisette Lopez, Lissette Lugo, Freddy Maldonado, Nelson Martinez, Fernando Mena, Ralph Mendez, Jerry Olavarria, Daniel Peralta, Jeff Perez, Gerald Rivera, John Rodriguez, Monique Rubio, Adelfi Delos Santos, Juan Sierra, Michael Toribio, Iris Torres, Leona Velazquez; Shaun Aldebot, Jennifer Amaro, Carol Burgos, Franklin de la Cruz, Reyson Dominguez, Jorge Gabino, Lisa Garcia, Anthony

Goenaga, Carlos Hernandez, Ilene La Torre, Ralph Mendez, Henry Perez, Hemitano Polanco, Alexis Ramirez, Rafael Reynoso, Efrain Rivera, Michael Toribio, Octavio Villacres; Phillip Barklay, Laura Blake, German Berges, William Chambers, Alfred Cruz, Gavin Eason, Johnny Guevera, Gregory Knox, Jean Mieses, Miguel Perez, Santa Quebas, David Soto, Elisea Trujillo, Taj Washington, Adam Wolowick; Mabel Batista, Laura Blake, Angel Codero, Eileen Diaz, Guarionex Dominguez, Lourdes Dominguez, Michelle Fernandez, Luis Heredia, Julie Mieses, Milina Marichal, Jaime Morales, Harold Navarro, Esteban Ramos, Maria Rincon, Marlena Rodriguez, Paula Rodriguez, Alexandra Torres, Suheilly Trivino, Caroll Vargas; Nelson Arias, Joshua Brito, Eben Broadbent, Karla Broady, Audrey Brown, Tarik Cranston, Zayd Dohrn, Melanie Duncan, Mahasin El Amin, Andy Febus, Theo Gangi, Latisha Gregg, Shameeka Harris, Anthony Johnson, Thai Jones, Carina Kalke, Nigel Martinez, Steven Melendez, Jessica Montanez, Orlando Munguia, Janelle Rivera, Ignacio Rodriguez, Arthur Schroeder, Kingsley Waring, Tamika Williams, Terron Williams, Alysa Wilson, Lauren Winfield; Cathy Burns, Savonna Campbell, Brandon Cohen, Jeremy Colangelo-Bryan, Jessica Cook-Mack, Pharoah Cranston, Flashaun Green, Jesse Greenbaum, Suavette Hagans, Josh Heisler, Dave Kaplan, Christopher Lee, Royston Nero, Sonya Shah, Jessica Ship, Elizabeth Van Benschoten, Aquila Washington, Ana Wolovick, Amana Woode.

Contents

A Personal Introduction

A TV Turn-Off is a simple experiment in which a group—a family, for instance, or a class, or even a whole school—agrees to go "cold turkey" from television for a limited period of time under certain controlled conditions. (The Turn-Off outlined in this book lasts for one week.)

The purpose of a Turn-Off is not to attack television or to create guilt about watching it. Rather, it is meant to help parents, teachers, and children better understand the role TV plays in their lives so that they can learn to control it more effectively. It is an experiment that has been tried successfully by quite a number of families and schools during the past ten or so years. In 1974, however, when I organized the Denver No-TV Experiment (quite possibly the first TV Turn-Off anywhere), I had no idea what to expect.

I was living in Colorado then, engaged simultaneously in two careers—being a writer, and raising kids. In pursuit of the first I had just signed up to write what I hoped would be my first big book. Not coincidentally, the subject I had chosen—television's effects on children and family life—was one that was causing me considerable uneasiness in my other career as parent.

It was not the programs my children watched that troubled me: rather, it was the strange, trancelike way they sat and stared at the TV set, regardless of what they were watching. I was also distressed by my own inability to resist "plugging them in" when I needed time for my work, no matter how guilty this made me feel. What's more, I sensed that television was affecting our family life—and not in a good way.

Since these concerns had nothing to do with *what* children watched on TV, I proposed to look into the television experience itself, rather than the programs that appear on TV. My plan was to find out what scientists and child experts were saying about this aspect of television viewing, both for my own guidance as a parent and for the purposes of my book. But after a few weeks at the library I made an uncomfortable discovery: the particular kind of scientific research I was counting on to form a substantial part of my book did not exist.

There were mountains of studies about the effects of viewing specific kinds of programs—violent or overstimulating or commercial—yet none of my questions about how the hours children spend watching television might change the way they develop or how the availability of television might affect child-rearing or family life were even raised, let alone answered.

The popular child experts of the day were similarly unhelpful: their writings too were focused entirely on the programs children watched. (This remains true today.) Gradually I began to realize that I had a difficult choice to make: either I would have to give up on a book I deeply believed needed writing, or I, a non-scientist, would have to initiate some research of my own. That's how the TV Turn-Off idea was invented—out of necessity.

In the spring of 1974, I prevailed upon the radio and television critic of the *Denver Post* to include in her column an invitation to families with young children: Are you worried about television's dominating role in your family? Come join an informal experiment that involves turning off your television sets entirely for a month.

Out of almost a hundred responses, fifteen families actually put away their TVs for at least a month, kept thorough diaries, and made themselves available for interviews before, during, and after the No-TV period. That, in a nutshell, was the Denver No-TV Experiment.

When I had read through the diaries of the No-TV families at the end of the experiment and concluded the first set of interviews with all participating parents and children, I was amazed at the results. I had expected a mixed reaction to the loss of television, but while most of the families experienced some difficulties at the beginning of the experiment ("the withdrawal period," as many called it), in every diary the reports on changes were enthusiastic, in some cases euphoric.

Among the improvements these families observed during the No-TV period were: better communication between children and adults; a more peaceful atmosphere in the home; a greater feeling of closeness as a family; more help around the house by the children; more leisurely meals with more interesting mealtime conversations; more reading by both parents and children; more real play among the children; improved relations between the parents themselves.

The negative aspects of the experiment were minor in comparison: parents and children missed favorite programs; some kids experienced a "weird" feeling without the television set on; and quite a few parents reported discipline problems without television deprivation to use as an ultimate threat.

A month later, however, when I return to each family for a follow-up interview, I was cast into a state of doubt about the experiment: if life had really been more enjoyable, marital relations more harmonious, and children's play more creative in the absence of television, then why, I asked myself, had every single family gone back to regular television watching at the end of the month?

"Since you had such a good experience during the experiment, did you ever consider giving up TV altogether?" I asked each family.

No, they all admitted a bit sheepishly, and offered a variety of explanations. "Television is here to stay," or "We have to learn to live with it," or "It would be too great a deprivation for the kids" were the most common ones.

It didn't make sense to me. Why should a family deliberately choose an inferior way of life over a better one they could easily obtain? Could I really trust those rhapsodic reports about life without TV? Perhaps people had reported what they thought I wanted to hear, or what they thought they *ought* to have felt rather than what had really happened when they turned off the television set.

I began to feel embarrassed about the whole thing myself. Obviously the Denver No-TV Experiment had been a failure. I shoved the great mass of papers into a cardboard carton, shoved it in the back of a closet, and then painfully shoved all thoughts of the project into that remote corner of my mind where other disappointments and failures lay decently buried. I proceeded to write my book without it.

I spent the next two and a half years interviewing hundreds of parents and children about television, struggling to understand their complicated relationships with that seductive medium. Only when my book, now titled *The Plug-In Drug,* was in the final stages of production did something tell me to look once again at the material I had collected from the Denver families. This time, I had a very different reaction.

As I read through the diaries and interviews, I began to see that the No-TV Experiment had been far from a failure for the families involved, even though they had not taken the extreme measure of eliminating television entirely from their homes. They had genuinely experienced gratifying changes during their Turn-Off and had gained some useful new insights. Some had begun to face an addictive pattern in the viewing of one or several family members—the first step in doing something about it. Others saw that television was eating into their family time far more than they had realized before the experiment. All came to recognize the need for greater television control and felt they were better equipped to achieve it now.

At last I was ready to understand the parents' embarrassed tone as they explained why they had gone back to life with television. Surely the conflict each of the Denver families faced as they resumed regular viewing was a manifestation of that universal struggle between activity and passivity, between independence and dependence, that lay at the very heart of the television problem I was writing about in my book.

Although it meant delaying publication, I went back to work and added a chapter incorporating the No-TV Experiment material. And I began to think about trying the experiment again, perhaps in a new way.

In 1977, I organized another No-TV Experiment—this one lasting a single week rather than a month and involving an entire school rather than scattered families in a community. No-TV Week at P.S. 166 (a public school in New York City) was a success. Hundreds of teachers and students, some on their own and some with their entire families, participated in the TV Turn-Off and attended the final party, where they told of the discoveries they had made during their week without television.

A number of outsiders attended the party as well, including

reporters from *The New York Times* and the *Daily News*. Several radio and TV stations sent crews to cover this "extraordinary" event. After that, often quite by chance, I began to hear of other schools as well as libraries and entire communities throughout the country that had organized and run successful TV Turn-Offs. Many of them mentioned No-TV Week at P.S. 166 as their inspiration. Clearly the idea was spreading throughout the country.

In 1985, I supervised another School Turn-Off in New York City. This one was at P.S. 84, the neighborhood school my own children had attended, and again, it proved to be an exciting and inspiring event. It was during this period that I began to think about writing a practical sort of book that would encourage and help parents, teachers, and schools organize successful TV Turn-Offs of their own. This, then, is that book.

A few words about organization:

The arguments and ideas in part I are intended to strengthen your resolve if you are considering the possibility of a Turn-Off but have not yet decided to "take the plunge." They will then help you "sell" the Turn-Off idea to others in turn.

Four basic TV Turn-Off plans are provided in the following sections; part II for families to try on their own, part III for a teacher and a classroom of 8–12-year-old kids, part IV for teachers in the early grades, and part V for a school-wide event. Part VI describes a number of variations on the Turn-Off idea. Readers of this book who are planning to try one of these plans might nevertheless benefit from looking through the other sections: some ideas and specific suggestions included in the Family Turn-Off section, for instance, might prove helpful to an organizer of a Classroom or a School Turn-Off.

The two-part appendix at the end of this book contains practical help for parents, teachers, or librarians who are going ahead and planning a real Turn-Off. The first part, the Turn-Off Survival Kit, provides a sales pitch for selling the Turn-Off idea to others, ideas for family occupations and recreations during the No-TV period, and some instructions for basic art activities to do at home with young children. The second part, Nuts and Bolts, provides the various charts and forms you will need to carry out the Turn-Off rituals and activities, as well as helpful pages for the use of Turn-

Off organizers—sample notices for parents' meetings, hints on how to run a meeting about television, model press releases, and so on.

Note: The names of the families described in the case histories have been changed to protect their privacy. Their stories, however, and all other names in this book, are real.

—MARIE WINN
New York City
May 1987

Part I

Why a TV Turn-Off

"I JUST WISH WE HAD NEVER STARTED"

"My problem with television began when Max was born and David was three years old," says Mary Taylor. The Taylors live near Baltimore, Maryland, where Albert Taylor works as an orchestra musician and Mary has a job as an editor for a small university press.

"After David was born, Albert and I used to talk a lot about child-rearing. We made all sorts of resolutions, as first parents often do. Our kids wouldn't be allowed to be rude. They'd have an early bedtime. We also felt quite strongly that we would not let our children do a lot of television watching.

"My first idea was to get rid of the television set altogether. That seemed the easiest way to prevent television from becoming a real problem in our family the way it was in the families of so many of our friends. The reason we didn't was that Albert loves watching sports on television. It's one of his greatest pleasures. I'm not that much of a TV watcher—I'm basically a reader—but there *are* some things like old movies and documentaries that both of us like to watch. And so we never considered getting rid of the set. We were only determined that our kids wouldn't become village 'vidiots.'

"When we just had one child, the set was almost never on before he went to bed at seven o'clock. But after our second child, Max, was born television became a temptation. It wasn't so much that my life became physically harder with two children to take care of. It was the emotional complexities that were so fatiguing. I couldn't help feeling that all the attention I paid the baby was somehow a betrayal of my first son. I've heard that this is a natural feeling for parents when their second child arrives. I badly wanted to make David happy in whatever ways I could, since I felt that the baby had brought only unhappiness into his life—at least so far.

"One day David came home from the house of another three-year-old all full of a television program he had watched there—I suppose it was 'Sesame Street.' Now it wasn't that he asked me to turn on our TV set. Somehow he didn't make a connection between that delightful program and the television set in our bedroom that was almost never on. But it certainly gave me the idea that I might turn the TV set on for David sometimes, since he seemed to like it so much.

"It was an enormous relief for me from then on to salt David away with the television set for an hour here and an hour there. He seemed totally happy watching television, so that I didn't feel at all anxious about devoting myself to the baby. It wasn't as if I had to coax him to watch. He leaped at the chance any time it was offered. And I began to offer it more and more. Soon I began to rely on those regular periods of time when David watched television. There was an hour and sometimes two in the morning, and another hour and a half around suppertime.

"But I did feel guilty about letting David watch TV—'letting' is the wrong word—encouraging him, because it was always I who reminded him that it was time for a program, always I who turned the set on.

"I would sometimes sit and watch television with him. That made me feel less guilty. I'd try to humanize the experience, somehow, to talk to him about it, to explain things, trying to *share* the experience. But that didn't really work. He watched television with a terrible intensity. I truly don't think he heard me when I tried to talk to him during a TV program.

"Of course it wasn't as if David watched television all day. We still did a lot of other things together, and he played outdoors a lot. But as time went on, television viewing simply settled into our lives as a regular thing. David seemed so keen on his programs that I didn't want to cut down on such an obvious pleasure.

"Once Max grew out of infancy, needless to say my feelings of guilt disappeared. It became quite clear that having a brother was an asset, that our whole family was enriched by the addition of that little character, and that, in fact, some of those guilt feelings had been more connected with my own anxieties than with anything real. But by then television was an established activity in the family, and by the time Max was two and a half he was a television watcher too. By that time, however, it wasn't me who turned on the set. It was David.

"I began to make real efforts to restrict TV watching, and sometimes they were successful. But I found that *I* had to supply substitute activities. I couldn't tell David 'Go play in your room,' without getting a lot of flack. And ever since I've gone back to work this year the situation has gotten much worse. The kids get home at three-thirty and a housekeeper looks after them until I get home at five-thirty, but I really can't keep her from letting them watch TV because they're more troublesome without it. And so I can only hope that the weather is nice and they'll be able to play outside. They're usually willing to do that. At most other times they come in and settle down with the TV set.

"Sometimes I threaten to get rid of the set. Albert agrees that the kids watch too much TV, so maybe we'll really do it. Or at least give it a try for a few months. The kids would probably be terribly angry at us if we did it, though. I just wish we had never started the whole thing in the first place! Everything would be a lot easier now."

The Trouble with Television

MOST PARENTS WORRY ABOUT TV— BUT NOT FOR THE RIGHT REASONS

My parents don't think I should watch as much TV as I do. They think a lot of the programs I watch are meaningless.

—Fifth grader, P.S. 84, No-TV Week

Of all the wonders of modern technology that have transformed family life during the last century, television stands alone as a universal source of parental anxiety. Few parents worry about how the electric light or the automobile or the telephone might alter their children's development. But most parents do worry about TV.

Parents worry most of all about the programs their children watch. If only these weren't so violent, so sexually explicit, so cynical, so *unsuitable,* if only they were more innocent, more educational, more *worthwhile.*

Imagine what would happen if suddenly, by some miracle, the only programs available on all channels at all hours of day and night were delightful, worthwhile shows that children love and parents wholeheartedly approve. Would this eliminate that nagging anxiety about television that troubles so many parents today?

For most families, the answer is no. After all, if programs were the only problem, there would be an obvious solution: turn the set off. The fact that parents leave the sets on even when they are distressed about programs reveals that television serves a number of purposes that have nothing to do with the programs on the screen.

Great numbers of parents today see television as a way to make child-rearing less burdensome. In the absence of Mother's Helper (a widely used nineteenth-century patent medicine that contained a hefty dose of the narcotic laudanum), there is nothing that keeps children out of trouble as reliably as "plugging them in."

Television serves families in other ways: as a time-filler ("You have nothing to do? Go watch TV"), a tranquilizer ("When the kids come home from school they're so keyed up that they need to watch for a while to simmer down"), a problem solver ("Kids, stop fighting. It's time for your program"), a procrastination device ("I'll just watch one more program before I do my homework"), a punishment ("If you don't stop teasing your little sister, no TV for a week"), and a reward ("If you get an A on your composition you can watch an extra hour of TV"). For parents and children alike it serves as an avoidance mechanism ("I can't discuss that now—I'm watching my program"), a substitute friend ("I need the TV on for company"), and an escape mechanism ("I'll turn on the TV and try to forget my worries").

Most families recognize the wonderful services that television has to offer. Few, however, are aware that there is a heavy price to pay. Here are eight significant ways television wields a negative influence on children and family life:

1. TV Keeps Families from Doing Other Things

> The primary danger of the television screen lies not so much in the behavior it produces—although there is danger there—as in the behavior it prevents: the talks, the games, the family festivities and arguments through which much of the child's learning takes place and through which his character is formed. Turning on the television set can turn off the process that transforms children into people.[1]

Urie Bronfenbrenner's words to a conference of educators almost two decades ago focus on what sociologists call the "reduc-

tion effects" of television—its power to preempt and often eliminate a whole range of other activities and experiences. While it is
easy to see that for a child who watches 32 hours of television each
week, the reduction effects are significant—obviously that child
would be spending 32 hours doing *something* else if there were no
television available—Bronfenbrenner's view remains an uncom-
mon and even an eccentric one.

Today the prevailing focus remains on improving programs
rather than on reducing the amount of time children view. Perhaps
parents have come to depend so deeply on television that they are
afraid even to contemplate the idea that something might be wrong
with their use of television, not merely with the programs on the
air.

2. TV Is a Hidden Competitor for All Other Activities

*Now that I couldn't watch TV I thought of other things
to do. I read all the books that I had classified as "boring" and discovered how good they really were.*
    —Sixth grader, Marshall, Missouri, Turn-Off

Almost everybody knows that there are better, more fulfilling
things for a family to do than watch television. And yet, if viewing
statistics are to be believed, most families spend most of their
family time together in front of the flickering screen.

Some social critics believe that television has come to dominate
family life because today's parents are too selfish and narcissistic
to put in the effort that reading aloud or playing games or even just
talking to each other would require. But this harsh judgment
doesn't take into consideration the extraordinary power of television. In reality, many parents crave a richer family life and are
eager to work at achieving this goal. The trouble is that their
children seem to reject all those fine family alternatives in favor of
television.

To be sure, the fact that children are likely to choose watching
television over having a story read aloud to them, or playing with a
stamp collection, or going out for a walk in the park does not
mean that watching television is actually more entertaining or gratifying than any of these activities. It does mean, however, that
watching television is easier.

In most families, television is always there as an easy and safe competitor. When another activity is proposed, it had better be *really special;* otherwise it is in danger of being rejected. The parents who have unsuccessfully proposed a game or a story end up feeling rejected as well. They are unaware that television is still affecting their children's enjoyment of other activities, even when the set is off.

Reading aloud is a good example of how this competition factor works. Virtually every child expert hails reading aloud as a delightful family pastime. Educators encourage it as an important way for parents to help their children develop a love for reading and improve their reading skills. Too often, however, the fantasy of the happy family gathered around to listen to a story is replaced by a different reality: "Hey kids, I've got a great book to read aloud. How about it?" says the parent. "Not now, Dad, we want to watch 'The Cosby Show,' " say the kids.

It is for this reason that one of the most important *Don'ts* suggested by Jim Trelease in his valuable guide *The Read Aloud Handbook* is the following:

> Don't try to compete with television. If you say, "Which do you want, a story or TV?" they will usually choose the latter. That is like saying to a 9-year-old, "Which do you want, vegetables or a donut?" Since *you* are the adult, *you* choose. "The television goes off at eight-thirty in this house. If you want a story before bed, that's fine. If not, that's fine too. But no television after eight-thirty." But don't let books appear to be responsible for depriving children of viewing time.[2]

3. TV Allows Kids to Grow Up Less Civilized

> *The Turn-Off showed us parents that we can say "no" without so many objections from the kids.*
> —Mother, Buffalo, New York, Great TV Turn-Off

It would be a mistake to assume that the basic child-rearing philosophy of parents of the past was stricter than that of parents today. American parents, in fact, have always had a tendency to be more egalitarian in their family life than, say, European parents.

For confirmation, one has only to read the accounts of eighteenth- or nineteenth-century European travelers who comment on the freedom and audacity of American children as compared to their European counterparts. Why then do parents today seem far less in control of their children than parents not only of the distant past but even of a mere generation ago? Television has surely played a part in this change.

Today's parents universally use television to keep their children occupied when they have work to do or when they need a break from child care. They can hardly imagine how parents survived before television. Yet parents *did* survive in the years before TV. Without television, they simply had to use different survival strategies to be able to cook dinner, talk on the telephone, clean house, or do whatever work needed to be done in peace.

Most of these strategies fell into the category social scientists refer to as "socialization"—the civilizing process that transforms small creatures intent upon the speedy gratification of their own instinctive needs and desires into successful members of a society in which those individual needs and desires must often be left ungratified, at least temporarily, for the good of the group.

What were these "socialization" strategies parents used to use? Generally, they went something like this: "Mommy's got to cook dinner now (make a phone call, talk to Mrs. Jones, etc.). Here are some blocks (some clay, a pair of blunt scissors and a magazine, etc.). Now you have to be a good girl and play by yourself for a while and not interrupt Mommy." Nothing very complicated.

But in order to succeed, a certain firmness was absolutely necessary, and parents knew it, even if asserting authority was not their preferred way of dealing with children. They knew they had to work steadily at "training" their child to behave in ways that allowed them to do those normal things that needed to be done. Actually, achieving this goal was not terribly difficult. It took a little effort to set up certain patterns—perhaps a few days or a week of patient but firm insistence that the child behave in certain ways at certain times. But parents of the past didn't agonize about whether this was going to be psychologically damaging. They simply had no choice. Certain things simply *had to be done,* and so parents stood their ground against children's natural struggle to gain attention and have their own way.

Obviously it is easier to get a break from child care by setting the child in front of the television set than to teach the child to play alone for certain periods of time. In the first case, the child is immediately amused (or hypnotized) by the program, and the parent has time to pursue other activities. Accustoming children to play alone, on the other hand, requires day-after-day perseverance, and neither parent nor child enjoys the process very much.

But there is an inevitable price to pay when a parent never has to be firm and authoritative, never has to use that "I mean business" tone of voice: socialization, that crucial process so necessary for the child's future as a successful member of a family, a school, a community, and a nation is accomplished less completely. A very different kind of relationship between parent and child is established, one in which the parent has little control over the child's behavior.

The consequences of a large-scale reduction in child socialization are not hard to see in contemporary society: an increased number of parents who feel helpless and out of control of their children's lives and behavior, who haven't established the parental authority that might protect their children from involvement in such dangerous activities as drug experimentation, or from the physical and emotional consequences of precocious sexual relationships.

4. Television Takes the Place of Play

> *I always used to turn the TV on for my 2½-year-old son Alexander in the morning. Then I noticed during No-TV week that he played in a different way all morning. He seemed less irritable—in a better mood—everything was entirely different. I realized it wasn't Alexander who wanted to watch TV—it was I who needed to turn it on for him.*
> —Parent, P.S. 84, New York City, No-TV Week

Once small children become able to concentrate on television and make some sense of it—usually around the end of their second year of life—it's not hard to understand why parents eagerly set their children before the flickering screen: taking care of toddlers is hard! The desperate and tired parent can't imagine *not* taking advantage of this marvelous new way to get a break. In consequence, before they are three years old, the opportunities of active play and exploration are hugely diminished for a great number of children—to be replaced by the hypnotic gratification of television viewing.

Yet many parents overlook an important fact: children who are suddenly able to sustain attention for more than a few minutes on the TV screen have clearly moved into a new stage of cognitive development—their ability to concentrate on TV is a sign of it. There are therefore many other new activities, far more developmentally valuable, that the child is now ready for. These are the simple forms of play that most small children enjoyed in the pre-television era: cutting and pasting, coloring and drawing, building with blocks, playing games of make-believe with toy soldiers or animals or dolls. But the parent who begins to fill in the child's time with television at this point is unlikely to discover these other potential capabilities.

It requires a bit of effort to establish new play routines—more effort, certainly, than plunking a child in front of a television screen, but not really a great deal. It requires a bit of patience to get the child accustomed to a new kind of play—play on his own—but again, not a very great deal. It also demands some firmness and perseverance. And a small amount of equipment (art materials, blocks, etc.), most of it cheap, if not free, and easily available.

But the benefits for both parent and child of *not* taking the easiest way out at this point by using television to ease the inevitable child-care burdens will vastly outweigh the temporary difficulties parents face in filling children's time with less passive activities. For the parent, the need for a bit more firmness leads to an easier, more controlled parent-child relationship. For the child, those play routines established in early childhood will develop into lifelong interests and hobbies, while the skills acquired in the course of play lead to a sense of accomplishment that could never have been achieved if the child had spent those hours "watching" instead of "doing."

5. TV Makes Children Less Resourceful

Tuesday I got home from school and didn't get to watch any of those old returns that I've seen a hundred times before. I did my homework right after school, then I practiced my clarinet and guitar.

—High school student, Richmond, Indiana, Turn-Off

Many parents who welcome the idea of turning off the TV and spending more time with the family are still worried that without TV they would constantly be on call as entertainers for their children. Though they *want* to play games and read aloud to their children, the idea of having to replace television minute-for-minute with worthwhile family activities is daunting. They remember thinking up all sorts of things to do when they were kids. But their own kids seem different, less resourceful, somehow. When there's nothing to do, these parents observe regretfully, their kids seem unable to come up with anything to do besides turning on the TV.

One father, for example, says, "When I was a kid, we were always thinking up things to do, projects and games. We certainly never whined to our parents, 'I have nothing to do!' " He compares this with his own children today: "They're simply lazy. If someone doesn't entertain them, they'll happily sit there watching TV all day."

There is one word for this father's disappointment: unfair. It is as if he were disappointed in them for not reading Greek though they have never studied the language. He deplores his children's lack of inventiveness, as if the ability to play were something innate that his children are missing. In fact, while the *tendency* to play is built into the human species, the actual *ability* to play—to imagine, to invent, to elaborate on reality in a playful way—and the ability to gain fulfillment from it, these are skills that have to be learned and developed.

Such disappointment, however, is not only unjust, it is also destructive. Sensing their parents' disappointment, children come to believe that they are, indeed, lacking something, and that this makes them less worthy of admiration and respect. Giving children the opportunity to develop new resources, to enlarge their horizons and discover the pleasures of doing things on their own is, on the other hand, a way to help children develop a confident feeling about themselves as capable and interesting people.

It is, of course, ironic that many parents avoid a TV Turn-Off out of fear that their children won't know what to do with themselves in the absence of television. It is television watching itself that has allowed them to grow up without learning how to be resourceful and television watching that keeps them from developing those skills that would enable them to fill in their empty time enjoyably.

6. TV Has a Negative Effect on Children's Physical Fitness

Dear Diary:
Today instead of TV I did exercises. I kicked my legs 50
times and jumped up and down 50 times. Then I took a
bath. Then I cut papers and drew. Then I did knitting five
times. It did not turn out so good.
—Fifth grader, P.S. 84, No-TV Week

Not long ago a study that attracted wide notice in the popular press found a direct relationship between the incidence of obesity in children and time spent viewing television. For the 6–11 age group, "children who watched more television experienced a greater prevalence of obesity, or superobesity, than children watching less television. No significant differences existed between obese, superobese, and nonobese children with respect to the number of friends, their ability to get along with friends, or time spent with friends, alone, listening to the radio, reading, or in leisure time activities," wrote the researchers. As for teenagers, only 10 percent of those teenagers who watched TV an hour or less a day were obese as compared to 20 percent of those who watched more than five hours daily. With most other variables eliminated, why should this be? The researchers provided a commonsense explanation: Dedicated TV watchers are fatter because they eat more and exercise less while glued to the tube.[3]

7. TV Has a Negative Effect on Children's School Achievement

One day my class was getting ready to have a science test.
There was nothing to do during the Turn-Off Week so I
studied instead. I got S − , a good grade. My parents
were proud of me.
—Fourth grader, Marshall, Missouri, Turn-Off

It is difficult if not impossible to prove that excessive television viewing has a direct negative effect on young children's cognitive development, though by using cautionary phrases such as "TV will turn your brain to mush" parents often express an instinctive belief that this is true.

Nevertheless an impressive number of research studies demon-

strate beyond any reasonable doubt that excessive television viewing has an adverse effect on children's achievement in school. One
study, for instance, shows that younger children who watch more
TV have lower scores in reading and overall achievement tests than
those who watch less TV.[4]

Another large-scale study, conducted when television was first
introduced as a mass medium in Japan, found that as families
acquired television sets children showed a decline in both reading
skills and homework time.

But it does not require costly research projects to demonstrate
that television viewing affects children's school work adversely.
Interviews with teachers who have participated in TV Turn-Offs
provide confirmation as well.

Almost without exception, these teachers testify that the quality
of homework brought into class during the No-TV period was
substantially better. As a fifth grade teacher noted: "There was a
real difference in the homework I was getting during No-TV
Week. Kids who usually do a good job on homework did a terrific
job. Some kids who rarely hand in assignments on time now
brought in surprisingly good and thorough work. When I brought
this to the class's attention during discussion time they said, 'Well,
there was nothing else to do!' "

8. Television Watching May Be a Serious Addiction

> *Every time I walked through the living room I longed to*
> *sit down, relax, and watch dumb reruns of TV. I think I*
> *was suffering from TV withdrawal symptoms. After a*
> *few days, though, I was used to doing other things with*
> *my time.*
>
> —Tenth grader, Marshall, Missouri, Turn-Off

A lot of people who have nothing but bad things to say about
TV, calling it the "idiot box" and the "boob tube," nevertheless
spend quite a lot of their free time watching television. People are
often apologetic, even shamefaced about their television viewing,
saying things like, "I only watch the news," or "I only turn the set
on for company," or "I only watch when I'm too tired to do
anything else" to explain the sizable number of hours they devote
to TV.

In addition to anxiety about their own viewing patterns, many parents recognize that their children watch too much television and that it is having an adverse effect on their development and yet they don't take any effective action to change the situation.

Why is there so much confusion, ambivalence, and self-deception connected with television viewing? One explanation is that great numbers of television viewers are to some degree addicted to the *experience* of watching television. The confusion and ambivalence they reveal about television may then be recognized as typical reactions of an addict unwilling to face an addiction or unable to get rid of it.

Most people find it hard to consider television viewing a serious addiction. Addictions to tobacco or alcohol, after all, are known to cause life-threatening diseases—lung cancer or cirrhosis of the liver. Drug addiction leads to dangerous behavioral aberrations—violence and crime. Meanwhile, the worst physiological consequences of television addiction seem to be a possible decline in overall physical fitness, and an increased incidence of obesity.

It is in its psychosocial consequences, especially its effects on relationships and family life, that television watching may be as damaging as chemical addiction. We all know the terrible toll alcoholism or drug addiction takes on the families of addicts. Is it possible that television watching has a similarly destructive potential for family life?

Most of us are at least dimly aware of the addictive power of television through our own experiences with the medium: our compulsive involvement with the tube too often keeps us from talking to each other, from doing things together, from working and learning and getting involved in community affairs. The hours we spend viewing prove to be curiously unfulfilling. We end up feeling depressed, though the program we've been watching was a comedy. And yet we cannot seem to turn the set off, or even *not* turn it on in the first place. Doesn't this sound like an addiction?

"A DRAMATIC CHANGE"

A few years ago I received the following letter from a woman in Denver who had read about my involvement with a No-TV Experiment:

"We are a family of four. My husband and I are in our thirties, our daughter is eleven, and our son eight years old. Until last October our children were typical TV addicts, even though I tried hard to limit the amount of TV they could watch. I had been very concerned about the effects of a lot of TV watching. I'd watch my daughter go into a trancelike state whenever the TV was on—it didn't matter what she was viewing. My son, much more active than his sister always, would often get up, leave the room, then return. However, as time went on, he too became totally passive in front of the set.

"For years my own reaction to this was a tremendous feeling of guilt, which led me to limit their viewing time to about two hours a day. Still, it was always a relief to me to have them quietly occupied with TV, especially during the winter months. I suppose I felt that a 'good mother' would find something else for them to do, but most times I felt I was too busy, or frankly resented having to try to occupy them. Also, I must mention, that Saturday mornings they were allowed to watch all the cartoons—and that amounted to a good deal more than two hours!

"About three years ago my husband and I had a serious break in our marriage and we were separated for three months. We worked out our problems, but one of the major decisions we made between us was to stop watching nighttime TV, unless there was something *really* special on. We realized that one of our problems was that we had stopped communicating with each other; at the end of nine years of marriage we had become strangers. (I don't mean to suggest that TV was the cause of this breakdown—only that we spent time together watching when we could have been spending time together *living*.)

"The immediate impact on the two of us was really dramatic. We both began to rediscover, through conversation, all of the delightful things that had led us to marriage in the first place. Meanwhile, the children were still allowed to watch their two hours. My husband works at least one night a week, and on those nights I'd also allow the TV to 'baby-sit' me until he got home at 9 P.M.

"Less than a year ago, on an evening when my husband was working, the three of us were watching TV when it *literally* caught on fire. It began smoking, and even though I unplugged it it continued to smoke and crackle. So I called the fire department and got us out of the house because the TV had started flaming and the smoke was unbearable. Soon four fire trucks arrived at our house. No damage was done to our house, but the TV set was ruined and beyond repair.

"After the excitement died down, the children's first concern was" '*What* are we going to do without the TV?' Withdrawal had already set in.

"We were going to be reimbursed somewhat by our insurance, (about $147), but it was an old set, and we really couldn't afford to replace it with another. And so my husband and I decided that we would *not* replace it—cold turkey! (We'd use the insurance reimbursement to buy crafts and games, we decided.)

"The first week was hard on all of us, especially the kids and me. They sort of 'hung around,' they didn't know what to do with themselves. I suggested reading, which we did a lot of, but still time was long sometimes. . . .

"Finally it began to get easier and easier for all of us and I can really say now that we don't miss it. We will not buy another set, either—we have really kicked the habit! I know that sometimes the kids watch something at their friends' homes, but it doesn't amount to much, and it certainly isn't addiction.

"The difference this has made in our lives is enormous! We had a wonderful winter, full of new discoveries of hidden talents and interests. I learned to needlepoint and my daughter learned macramé. My husband has done a lot of cabinet work in the house, while listening to his favorite sports programs on the radio. When we had the TV, he used to watch all Sunday until he was glassy-eyed. He's also started oil painting. We've done a lot of reading aloud in front of the fireplace. We have much longer dinners now since nobody is hurrying to watch TV programs, and sometimes we eat by candlelight—the kids love it!

"We are really a *family* again—united by common experiences and bonds. It's a wonderful feeling. Frequently each of us is asked if we saw such-and-such on TV last night and we can't respond very well, but we've gotten used to that.

"I don't know if any of this long story is useful to you, but I was really inspired to read of your experiment and I hope you receive a lot of support from the community."

·2·

How a Turn-Off, Though Temporary, Can Make a Real Difference

CASTING A NEW LIGHT ON TELEVISION

I didn't realize how much I use the TV to entertain the kids and keep them quiet. I was amazed at how creative the girls were when TV was not an option.
—Parent, Marshall, Missouri, Turn-Off

Television's negative influence on child-rearing and family life is difficult to demonstrate. How can anyone prove that those wonderful activities, those talks and games and family festivities would really happen if there were no TV? How can anyone show that if television was not available to parents as a child-rearing strategy, children would grow up to be more civilized, easier to live with?

There are, in fact, several ways to get a glimpse of that mysterious period of "non-time" during which certain activities—reading, practicing musical instruments, playing games, having conversations—don't happen because television is available as an easy substitute. One way is to talk to people who grew up before television came into the home, or to read about families in that bygone era. Such investigations often suggest that television has had a diminishing effect on family life.

A TV Turn-Off is a more persuasive way to uncover television's actual effects on today's family—on your family, to be specific. Observing the changes that occur during the No-TV period will cast light on the actual, and often hidden, effects of television on your family life and on your children's behavior.

Does the idea of a week without television make you uneasy, even fearful? This, in fact, is evidence that television is not a simple entertainment for you. It is a habit, and possibly an addiction. The changes that occur during a TV Turn-Off may be a revelation. As a more fulfilling way of life sets in, you may begin to wonder why the pleasures of watching TV had once seemed so great—when life without it is so remarkably improved. This often proves to be the crucial first step in doing something decisive about a serious addiction.

THE GOOD-ENOUGH FAMILY

When we turned off the TV we were able to spend more time together as a family. This was something we always talked about doing but never seemed to get around to it. By signing the pledge we put action to our words.
—Mother, Great TV Turn-Off, Buffalo, New York

All families are not created equal. Some families seem to be spectacularly successful. Others are a total mess. And then somewhere between the heights and the depths are most of the rest of us.

A TV Turn-Off is not particularly useful for those families at the two extremes of this spectrum. Mr. and Mrs. Spectacular seem to have such comfortable control over their children's lives that they don't even need to establish rules about television watching. Their children are too busy putting on plays, making up games and activities, drawing, painting, writing, and reading to even feel the pull of television. Family relations are so rich and harmonious that nobody ever wants to escape into the painless unrealities of television. Television never takes precedence over human activities—conversations, games, leisurely meals, reading aloud—in this somewhat unreal family.

The troubled families at the other extreme, unfortunately, are all too real: parents who don't get along with each other or who have already split up, who don't understand the first thing about children and their needs, who are too immature, too disturbed, too self-absorbed to place any great value on family life, and whose children, consequently, are likely to have more than the usual share of difficulties. Though excessive television watching is a common symptom of family pathology, these families are not likely to find that watching less television is going to make much of a difference in their lives. They have too many other basic problems to deal with first.

The British psychiatrist D. W. Winnicott once coined the phrase "good-enough mother" to describe a parent who may have considerable problems raising her children, but who still does a good enough job to avoid causing any serious psychological damage.[5] Similarly, one might define a "good-enough family" as one neither so perfect as to be invulnerable to normal human weaknesses and temptations nor so precariously balanced as to be swamped by its troubles. The good-enough family may have its shortcomings; nevertheless the parents care deeply about their children's well-being and strive to make their family life as good as possible.

There is, however, a wide range of these "good-enough" families: some might be called "better-than-good-enough," indeed, approaching the borders of "Spectacular" territory; others are "barely-good-enough," rapidly heading for deep trouble. For many of these families, the role television plays in their lives may decisively influence whether they go in one direction or the other. For them, a TV Turn-Off can be the first step in bringing about a permanent improvement in the quality of their daily life.

CAN A FAMILY WITH TWO WORKING PARENTS BENEFIT FROM A TURN-OFF?

As working parents my husband and I are sometimes tired and we forget our girls are really interesting to talk to and with. In a lot of ways I hated to see the TV Turn-Off end. Thanks for putting our family closer together.
—Letter to organizer, Richmond, Indiana, Turn-Off

For that growing number of families with two working parents the danger of television dependency is especially great. When the parents come home at the end of the day, the children, especially preschoolers, are likely to crave attention—it's only natural, after all. Unfortunately, after a hard day's work, the exhausted parents would like nothing better than to collapse in front of the tube for a few relaxing hours of passive entertainment.

Time, however, is a precious commodity for such families. They have available to them only those few evening hours, and the weekends, for that accumulation of experiences—the conversations, the rituals, the games, the books read aloud, the jokes, the plans, and even the squabbles and confrontations that lead to new understandings and adjustments—that help make a family something more than a random collection of people who happen to share the same house. Television watching, while often entertaining and relaxing, is a poor substitute for all those human activities.

For such families, a Turn-Off provides an opportunity to discover that they do not *need* television to survive the rigors of their complicated but often satisfying life—that, indeed, television may actually be making their lives more fragmented and frantic rather than more relaxed and easier. It will demonstrate that there are other ways to "unwind" after a day of work that are far more conducive to real family happiness than spacing out in front of the TV.

IS A TURN-OFF ADVISABLE IN A SINGLE-PARENT HOUSEHOLD?

Being a single parent who works two jobs, I hadn't realized that I was losing ground with my children. The Turn-Off helped me realize that we needed to spend more time together and get to know each other. My children and I have decided that we'll have no TV in our house two nights a week. Those will be our days to be a family.
—Post-Turn-Off survey, Marshall, Missouri

While parents in single-parent families generally have a more difficult time of it than parents in two-parent families, in the area of television control the situation is often quite the reverse. A single parent who decides that the kids are watching too much television can establish more stringent rules without the additional problem of getting a spouse to go along with it. Similarly, a single parent can decide on a Turn-Off without running into resistance from a fellow parent who *must* watch a favorite program.

Fatigue and loneliness, however—conditions endemic to single parents—along with anxiety, depression, and other more universal ills, often stand in the way of television control; the beleaguered parent feels that turning the set off and planning less passive activities would require more physical and mental energy than seems available.

In fact, using television as an escape from the very real problems that face a single parent will only perpetuate those problems. Meanwhile, the changes that occur naturally without television—a richer social life, more communication between parent and children, more involvement in sports and outdoor play, a new interest in taking trips and going places—are the very steps that may lead to a more fulfilling life for a single-parent family.

CAN TV KIDS STILL LEARN TO PLAY?

I honestly believe my four-year-old learned to play much more by herself during No-TV Week, and I'm going to encourage that. I'm not saying she'll never watch again. But I will make every effort never to stop any play time because it's time for a TV program.
—Parent, P.S. 166, New York City, No-TV Week

Parents who recognize that their children's long involvement with television has affected their ability to play and entertain themselves often despair of doing anything about it. It seems too difficult and too late to start teaching their children how to play and be resourceful.

Fortunately, children rarely need to start from scratch in learning how to play, even those who have been watching huge amounts of television from early childhood on. This is because Nature, in her infinite wisdom, has so arranged things that for quite a long period of time babies and very young children simply will not watch television with any sustained interest. And there's no way to force them to watch.

What they do instead is babble, sing, talk, touch, get into things, throw, climb, crawl, walk, jump, and engage in any number of other instinctive behaviors all aimed at acquiring more and more active experience. That is, they play.

The experiences of those early pre-television years form the vital underpinning of all later play and fantasy. And parents are the perfect educators at this stage, teaching instinctively almost from their baby's birth when they cuddle and dandle, when they play peekaboo and pattycake and "This Little Piggy Went to Market," when they talk and sing and tell stories just the way their own parents did.

But while those years are particularly crucial to children's development of play skills, they are also particularly trying years for parents. The sad truth is that if babies were willing and able to sit and watch television for hours at a time parents and caretakers would be unable to resist the temptation to make their own lives easier by "plugging them in."

Luckily, children will always have at least two full years of grace before television has a chance to affect their development. And even when the skills that each child develops during infancy and early childhood fall into disuse as the child begins to spend increasing amounts of time with television, they remain latent. It actually doesn't take much to reactivate them, as parents are amazed to discover during the course of a TV Turn-Off.

DECIDING TO TAKE THE PLUNGE

My family participated in No-TV Week and it was the best thing that ever happened to us.
—Kindergarten teacher, P.S. 84, New York City, No-TV Week

The arguments for using television only as an occasional entertainment rather than allowing it to become a habitual time-filler are powerful indeed. Nevertheless, the human capacity for avoiding a confrontation with unpleasant realities is equally powerful. Television has become so entrenched in the home and so intricately interwoven in the fabric of family life that resistance is particularly strong to the unpleasant possibility that the medium may, indeed, be having a harmful effect on children and family life.

But the mounting evidence of television's negative influence is persuasive enough to shake up the most entrenched users of television and cause them to want to find out for themselves whether TV is having a harmful effect on their children's development and on their family life.

Go ahead and take the plunge! It's only a week, after all. It might prove to be the most important week of your life.

· Part II ·

The Family Turn-Off

A GOOD FAMILY GETS BETTER

The Bells are a family with a lot going for them—a good marriage, bright, healthy children, a comfortable economic situation, and a knack for sound child-rearing. The family is close and active and—often the case with such successful families—aware of its areas of strength and weakness, working hard at emphasizing one and eliminating the other. The parents perceive their children's television patterns as a distinct area of weakness—that was their reason for joining a TV Turn-Off for an entire summer.

"Last June I got so fed up with the kids' insane mania for TV that when I heard about the experiment I announced that we were joining for the whole summer," Helen Bell wrote to me a few years ago. "My children are Tammy and Kate, age 10½ and 7½. Tammy likes TV but Kate is the real watcher. She'd watch all the time if we let her. I have to admit that often if I get started watching I find it hard to turn the darn thing off and will watch mindlessly some boring thing for no reason at all. Since banishing the kids, I've decided to take the cure, too."

Here are some excerpts from Helen Bell's Turn-Off diary, describing the first week of their Turn-Off:

"At first it was easy to keep the set off. But around Wednesday 'withdrawal' symptoms set in. Kids: 'May we watch "The Cosby

Show?" ' Mom: 'No.' Kids: 'Why? it's only a half hour!' Mom: 'No.' Kids: 'Oh, pleeese!' Mom: 'No.' Score: Mom—1, Kids—0."

How did a TV Turn-Off affect a family that didn't seem to have a serious addiction problem to begin with, and that seemed to be functioning well as a family? Surprisingly, the parents felt as great a difference in their family life when television was turned off as parents in families with serious addiction problems. Every aspect of family life was affected, according to the parents.

"It was painful at first," wrote Helen Bell, "but after the first week we were off and running. I've been teaching Tammy to sew. Kate's been trying her hand at some cooking. One cake pan turned upside down in the bottom of the stove—ooh, that was messy. That has to happen once when you're learning. And we're still all laughing our heads off when we look back at it."

As the summer progressed, the catalog of improvements continued. "The kids seem sort of proud of the fact that they can really entertain themselves. They both like to draw a lot and they made a request to Santa for some pastels this Christmas. We already have watercolors and oils. They both show an inclination towards art. They may not be good but they get a lot of pleasure from it," wrote Helen Bell during the fifth week of the experiment.

"Music, too, has become more important without the competition of TV. Both girls spend more time practicing their instruments (piano and violin) and now they even spend time playing together.

"Without the TV, the kids are much more willing to help me in the kitchen, both before and after dinner. I'm definitely not planning to get the dishwasher repaired, because we do a lot of talking these days while washing dishes, which we've never done before. With the dishwasher, we just threw the dishes in and walked off. But now we're working for ten, fifteen minutes together, and we really talk together, about what happened during the day, what so and so said to somebody else—it's just a comfortable sort of time, and maybe the warm, soapy water makes it easier to really talk.

"I really feel the family is pulling together tighter as a result of our Turn-Off. I know my husband feels this way just as strongly as I do. When we see the girls doing something new we'll say to each other: 'See, if we had the TV they wouldn't be doing this.'

"And there's a real difference about going outside. In the past we couldn't get the kids outside to save our souls unless Dick held the door and I booted them out, practically. Now they're going out in all sorts of weather, we have to yell after them to put on their boots. It used to be that *we'd* go out and build a snowman and they'd watch us from the living room. Now, I don't know, they just seem a lot hardier."

Helen Bell does not feel that her life as a parent has been made harder by the absence of TV. But she looks back to the time when her children were younger and wonders how she would have managed then.

"I remember when the children were little, and they'd get into things and television was just a great distracter. I certainly used it, and I'm sure if I had a little toddler around today I'd be terribly tempted. My kids today are of an age where I can say 'No, you can't watch TV. Go read a book. Go find something to do'—and they'll do it! In fact, they don't even ask anymore."

The Bells' experience provides an answer to the perennial questions: "What's so bad about kids watching television in their free time? Why can't kids just relax and be entertained?"

The alternative activities Tammy and Kate found themselves engaged in during the Turn-Off were enriching in ways television watching is not. A childhood spent gaining skills at art and music, playing and reading, paves the way for a fulfilling adulthood. A person who has learned, through a childhood of accumulated experiences, to initiate activities, to create opportunities for entertainment rather than to wait to be entertained will surely have a richer life than one without such acquired skills.

After the summer, the Bells went back to a more controlled way of life with TV. They moved the set from the living room to the basement to make viewing less comfortable and automatic. They tried (with fairly good success) to limit their viewing to special programs and weekends. They continue to look back at their summer-long Turn-Off as a particularly great family experience.

Get Ready:
Selling the Turn-Off
to Family and Friends

SETTING THE DATE

Now that you've decided to go ahead with the Turn-Off, the first decision is at hand: setting the date. Is one season better than another for a No-TV Experiment? Scheduling a Turn-Off in the spring or fall, when the weather is good enough for outdoor play, will probably make life easier for parents and children both. On the other hand, having a Turn-Off in the heart of winter, when the family is really thrown on its own resources, does illuminate most clearly the powerful hold television has on so many people's lives. Since it's a bit of a toss-up, the best idea is to go ahead and set it soon, whatever the season is now, before you lose the momentum of your present enthusiasm for the idea.

There are, however, a few times to avoid when scheduling a Turn-Off, especially if you are in any way dependent on television for relief from child care. Here are some guidelines for when *not* to schedule a Family Turn-Off:

1. During vacations

Since many families look forward to spending more time doing things together during vacations, it seems logical to consider scheduling a TV Turn-Off during a vacation. And, indeed, many families enjoy a natural TV Turn-Off during vacations, simply by traveling to places where there is no television set to turn on.

But trying a TV Turn-Off during a vacation at home where television is normally available is another matter. For a family accustomed to gaining respite from child care and child demands by using television, going "cold turkey" when there is a great deal of extra time on everybody's hands is just *too hard*. It may be a goal for the future, once new free-time patterns—playing, reading, writing—have been established in your family, but until then it makes more sense to schedule a TV Turn-Off during a time when life is at its most regular—when children have school and parents have work. (See chapter 6, "How *Not* to Do a Family TV Turn-Off," for a case study of how one family's lack of planning led to disaster.)

2. The week of a special sports or TV event—the World Series, a long-awaited TV special, a space launching, etc.

3. A week that promises to be stressful at a parent's workplace, or at school—such as exam or graduation week.

4. The busy, exciting week just before a major holiday.

"EXPLAINING" THE TURN-OFF TO TODDLERS

Many parents worry about how their toddlers will manage if they are suddenly deprived of their regular daily television programs. How can they explain the Turn-Off to them? "My Sammy just loves 'Sesame Street' and 'Mr. Rogers,' " one mother says of her two-year-old, "I'm sure he'd hate to miss them."

Two-year-old Sammy, in fact, is unlikely to take much notice of the absence of television during a Turn-Off. Preschoolers rarely *ask* to watch television, though they may actually spend many hours viewing. Since most two- and three-year-olds have a very vague sense of time, it is invariably the parent who knows what programs are on at what time and who turns the television set on for the child.

Nevertheless, anxiety about depriving toddlers of their "favorite" television programs is common among parents such as Sammy's mother. Odds are that it is an example of what psychologists call "projection"—the transferring of feelings or emotions one does not particularly want to face onto some other person. It is not so much Sammy who will suffer when the television program is turned off. It is his mother who'd "hate to miss" having him watch those programs that have been providing her with a regular respite from the rigors of child care. Besides, she may have enjoyed watching "Sesame Street" herself.

It is not necessary, or even desirable, to include a preschool child in any of the planning stages of a Turn-Off. It is certainly inadvisable to seek a young child's approval of a Turn-Off, as parents are encouraged to do with school-age or teen-age children. But it is not unlikely that a toddler will ask to watch TV sometime during the No-TV period. At that point a very matter-of-fact "We can't watch TV this week, so let's find something else to do" is the proper response.

SELLING THE TURN-OFF TO YOUR SCHOOL-AGE KIDS

How the idea of a Turn-Off is presented to the older children of the family is critical to its success. What can parents do to avoid being faced with a resentful and mutinous little gang who will do everything in their power to sabotage the experiment? Here are seven strategies for presenting a Turn-Off to children in the 6–12 age group.

1. *It's a Scientific Experiment:*
Emphasize the Turn-Off's importance as a scientific experiment. A TV Turn-Off is a genuine before-and-after study, a simple, yet legitimate research tool for social scientists. The data collected by each family if carefully kept and sent in according to the directions at the end of this book (see page 184) can add to scientist's understanding of television's role in school and family life.

Children who might under other circumstances consider the idea of a week without television a punishment are often interested enough in being part of a serious experiment to drop their defenses and have a positive attitude toward the Turn-Off.

2. *"We're All in This Together"*
The "We're all in this together" strategy is more likely to succeed with kids than the "this is for your own good" approach. Present the Turn-Off as an adventure for all participants, parents and children alike. It should not be presented as something that will improve kids' work habits, or turn them into readers, even though this is often the idea that motivates parents and teachers to try the experiment.

Even when the adults involved really don't watch very much

television, it helps if they admit to the children at the start of a Turn-Off, as dramatically as they truthfully can, that they will miss their favorite programs, and might find some aspects of the Turn-Off difficult.

3. Take the Turn-Off Challenge

Present the Turn-Off as a challenge, as an adventure, as a test— Can we survive two weeks without television?

4. Something New and Different

Emphasize the special nature of the Turn-Off—that there will be a new and different quality to life during it. Even if children have actually experienced periods of time without television, on vacations, say, or when TV deprivation was used as a punishment, this will be different. Don't forget that children who have been watching television steadily from their earliest years are often somewhat bored with it—even by their favorite programs. A real change in life, even one that presents difficulties such as a Turn-Off, can be exciting.

5. It's Not a Punishment

Above all, avoid having a Turn-Off seem to be a punishment. Since many families use "No TV" as a threat and then the ultimate punishment, it is not easy to keep the kids from feeling that a Turn-Off is also a punishment. This is why it is particularly important that older children's participation in a Turn-Off is voluntary. The fact that the family or class or school is taking part in it together is the crucial difference—it is this that holds out the promise that the Turn-Off might actually be fun. Another important difference between a Turn-Off and TV deprivation as punishment is the promised reward at the end.

6. A Reward

Knowing that there will be a reward for successful completion of the Turn-Off is a most important psychological spur to children who really *want* to join a Turn-Off but feel somewhat compelled to resist. The reward is certainly not a bribe—few children will decide to join a Turn-Off because of a promised reward. Rather, it is the *idea* of a reward for having done something difficult and worthwhile that pleases children.

7. Self-discovery

The wish for self-improvement is by no means an exclusively adult phenomenon. Children are often excited by the idea of discovering new capabilities, skills, and talents during the course of a Turn-Off. "You never know—you may think up an invention that will change the world," or "You might write a hit song or a great story or discover new interests that may actually change your whole life"—these are some of the approaches to a Turn-Off that might work.

WHAT IF THE KIDS STILL SAY NO

How are parents to proceed if they are convinced that a Turn-Off will be a valuable experience but the kids continue to be negative about the idea? Can the parents insist on going ahead, with the kids kicking and screaming all the way?

The answer to this question depends a good deal on each family's particular style of decision-making. Some parents have already established an easy and authoritative style of running the family. When a decision must be made, the parents give the kids a certain amount of leeway for their individual tastes and wishes (after all, being authoritative is very different from being authoritarian), but basic decisions are generally not subject to debate; they are firmly made by the parents. For instance, the parents decide that everyone in the family will help with the household chores, but the children may negotiate which chore they will take on, and what time of day they will do it.

Other parents who are less confident of their own adult authority have fallen into the habit of making joint decisions with their children, even very young ones. "Do you want to eat your dinner?" or "Do you want to go out to the playground?" or "Do you want to get ready for school now?" is the usual way they communicate their desires to their children, when they actually mean "It's time to eat dinner now" or "We're going out to the playground now" or "Please get ready for school or you'll be late."

Children from authoritative-style families are accustomed to accepting most parental decisions since these are rarely up for negotiation. They are not likely to reject the idea of a Turn-Off that has been presented to them in a positive way. If they are given a chance to join in on the planning, they are unlikely to feel that they have been forced to join against their will.

Children from the joint-decision-making-style families, on the other hand, often use each decision as an opportunity to test their power in the family. Obviously they are not always negative about *everything*—they will probably agree if asked if they want to go to the movies or want to go out and get ice-cream sundaes. But if the decision involves something a bit difficult, something that might be "good for them" but not necessarily fun, they are far more likely to reject it out of hand.

Firm parents will still profit by "selling" a TV Turn-Off to their children, holding out a desirable reward at the end, and emphasizing the adventure and challenge of a Turn-Off. They understand that it is important to help the children have a positive attitude toward this family experiment. They start, however, with the advantage of knowing that their children will probably accept the idea of the Turn-Off, just as their children have become used to accepting most other parental decisions.

But what about the joint-decision-makers? They cannot suddenly metamorphose into firm and authoritative parents, can they? What if they have tried their best to convince their children of all the benefits of a TV Turn-Off and the kids respond: "Not on your life! We're not going to join in!"

One approach, if the children have rejected the idea of a Turn-Off, is to tell them that you—the parent or parents—are going to go ahead with the Turn-Off anyway, because you are concerned about your own viewing patterns, and that even though you wish they would join you, you are not going to force them. They can continue to watch. But, you tell them, you would hope that they will at least help you out with your Turn-Off by only watching when you aren't around, and maybe watching less so that they can help *you* pass the time during the Turn-Off.

The consequence of this low-key approach is often that the children, having won the power struggle, and realizing that they're not going to be coerced into joining the Turn-Off, will end up joining it anyway, to all intents and purposes. Having the parents not watching TV is often perceived by the children as an opportunity for more personal time with and attention from the parents. And having parents in a situation where they say they need the children's help—such as having trouble adjusting to life without television, or missing their favorite program—is likely to inspire the children to join their parents in some of those alternative activities that are the very reason that the parents wanted the kids to join the Turn-Off in the first place.

Without being in any way dishonest, parents will probably do well to emphasize and even slightly exaggerate their difficulties in facing a week without television. As it happens, for great numbers of parents who have participated in Turn-Offs these difficulties turn out to be very real, and often far greater than they ever expected before the Turn-Off.

GETTING THE OTHER PARENT TO GO ALONG

Last spring I made a survey of all the kids in the third grade about whether they would cooperate in a TV Turn-Off. A lot of kids responded: "My Dad wouldn't let me turn off 'Miami Vice,' " or "My father would never give up 'Monday Night Football.' "
—Organizer of the Marshall, Missouri, TV Turn-Off

"I'd love to try a TV Turn-Off, but my husband (or wife) would never go along!" is a common complaint among parents. Here are four possible strategies that might be helpful in dealing with the problem of a resistant and possibly videoholic spouse (let's say it's the husband in this case):
1. (It may seem like wishful thinking, but it really happens this way sometimes!): Confidently present the idea to him, giving all the reasons why you think it would be valuable for the children and for the family (see summary of TV's negative effects, Appendix, p. 154). Instead of outright rejection, he may surprise you by agreeing. The "cold turkey" aspect of a temporary but total Turn-Off may be psychologically easier for an addict to handle than a "gradual reduction" approach.
2. Instead of dwelling on his "addiction problem," emphasize the benefits of a Turn-Off for the children—that it will favorably influence their behavior, their schoolwork, and their social and cognitive development. (See chapter 1 for ammunition.) This is strategically more effective and less likely to lead to immediate rejection than the frontal attack of "You're a TV junkie."

3. Make a straightforward deal: if he will cooperate in the Turn-Off, then you will . . .? (whatever it takes: come home earlier from work regularly; finally go on a diet; take that course you've put off taking). In other words, find your own area of weakness and use it as a bargaining tool.

4. If you don't receive out-and-out cooperation, at least try for a show of parental solidarity in front of the children. If a resistant husband, for instance, while making no promises of joining a Turn-Off himself, at least agrees to wholeheartedly support it for the children, he will usually end up watching far less than his normal amount of television. Why? Partly out of admiration for the strength of will of the other family members; partly, perhaps, to show his own strength of will as well; and partly because some of the other things going on during a Turn-Off may entice him away from his regular television programs.

GET COMPANY FOR YOUR TURN-OFF

Doing a Turn-Off entirely on your own as a family can be hard, especially if your family is small. Ideally, having one or more other families join in a Turn-Off makes it far more enjoyable for everybody concerned. This is the idea behind the larger scale Turn-Offs that include whole classes, schools, or even communities. Families who don't have the opportunity to be part of such large-scale enterprises yet wish to try a Turn-Off are encouraged to enlist at least one neighbor or friend in the project.

A good way to find company for a Turn-Off is to convince one of your children's teachers to organize a Classroom Turn-Off for the whole class. Discuss the idea with the teacher, using the arguments in "What's Wrong with Watching TV?," or "Why a TV Turn-Off" in the Appendix (pages 154 and 155).

·4·

Get Set:
Special Rituals and Activities

MAKE IT AN EVENT

A Turn-Off is not merely a time when television is eliminated. It is an opportunity for a family to redefine itself in certain ways, to expand its horizons, and to emphasize its common goals and aspirations. But in order to achieve these goals, all family members must see it as a special event, an adventure, a challenge rather than as a punishment and a deprivation.

It is important, therefore, to make the Turn-Off as distinctive and amusing as possible by setting up some specific rituals in preparation for the event. All the following activities work toward the goal of making the Turn-Off *a real event,* something important and out of the ordinary, something to pay special attention to. Only in this way, I believe, can one compensate from the start for the genuine and complicated loss of passive pleasure that a Turn-Off involves.

TURN-OFF RITUALS

Family rituals have been weakened and in many cases eliminated by the universal use of television as a family time-filler. A TV Turn-Off is a perfect time to begin working at the restoration of such rituals—those regular, repeated, sometimes silly but always delightful ceremonies, games, songs, parties, and routines that help to define the uniqueness and individuality of every family. The following rituals connected with the Turn-Off itself are a step in that direction. In addition, the rituals themselves are amusing and serve to make the Turn-Off a real event, one with a beginning, middle, and end.

1. The Contract

Signing a binding "contract" that spells out the conditions of the Turn-Off is a dramatic way to begin a Family Turn-Off. On the evening before the Turn-Off begins, bring out the document with a certain amount of ceremony, perhaps at the end of a family meal. Each family member then solemnly signs at the bottom of the contract. Mealtime "toasts" of farewell to TV and favorite programs are all dramatic flourishes that help children maintain a spirit of fun about the No-TV period.

Some low-key families might feel self-conscious about the idea of a formal contract. Parents of older children often worry that the kids will find the whole thing too "uncool." Of course you as a parent must do what you believe best suits your own family. But since the Turn-Off is intended to broaden and enrich family life, trying something a bit different during the course of it—such as bringing out a legal-looking contract for a ceremonial signing—is worth a try. Your kids may surprise you by throwing themselves into the experiment with enthusiasm.

A sample contract for parents and older children may be found on page 175 and a simpler version for younger children on page 174).

2. The Battle Plan

For many family members, time is likely to hang heavy during the Turn-Off period. Not everyone, to be sure, will have equal problems facing a week without television. Often there is one person in a family who is an addict to some degree, while others are far more casual about their watching—they can take it or leave it.

A Turn-Off Battle Plan session can help all members of the family deal with their different needs in relation to television. This is the time when parents and children come out in the open about their anxieties regarding the Turn-Off. With a notepad and pencil in hand, each family member figures out when television will be missed the most and makes special plans for those times.

Some children, for instance, are accustomed to turning on the TV the moment they come home from school to help them "wind down." (Try the phonograph instead.) Other family members are very involved with daytime serials and are unhappy at the thought of missing a few episodes. (Schedule a social visit with a friend who can fill you in.) A parent may worry about missing the evening news (Catch it on the radio) and may even be anxious about being unprepared to discuss important issues with work colleagues the next day (Read newspapers). These are the times that call for advance planning.

Obviously parents and kids may stray from their detailed Battle Plans when the actual Turn-Off week arrives. Nevertheless, many kids enjoy the idea of making an hour-by-hour schedule, and also enjoy sticking to it during the Turn-Off. And surely *some* of the substitute activities are more likely to take place if they have been planned in advance.

In addition to specific ideas for filling in time for individual family members, the Battle Plan should include some group activities for times the whole family is together—after dinner, for instance, or on the weekend. A model Battle Plan form appears on page 169 of the appendix. Make a copy for each family member.

3. The Family Viewing Chart

Keeping a Family Viewing Chart for a week before the Turn-Off can be a vital first step toward effective family television control. It is not unlike those reducing diets that require you to keep track of everything you eat for a week before commencing the actual regime. Many people find that the very act of writing down every item of food they eat acts as a strong inhibitor to overeating—they often lose more weight before the diet begins than they do during any week of the official diet period.

With television viewing, as with eating, people are often quite unaware of how much they actually "consume" each day. Many people who believe that they hardly watch television at all find to their amazement that when they keep track of every single time they turn on the television set it adds up to a good many hours.

At the start of the week before the Turn-Off place a Family Viewing Chart on top of each TV set in the house and make note of every program or portion of program watched by each member of the family. Parents should mark down what the youngest children watch—the rest of the family can keep track of their own watching. At the end of the week make an Individual Viewing

Chart for each family member. This will give you a clear picture of every individual's particular viewing patterns. There is a model Family Viewing Chart on page 168 you may copy and use.

4. A Special Trip to the Library

An indispensable part of the preparation for a TV Turn-Off is a family trip to the library. Having a stockpile of books ready for the Turn-Off serves as a sort of security blanket for many family members who may fight a feeling of panic at the idea of going "cold turkey."

If your family makes regular visits to the library, this one should be a special "TV Turn-Off Trip," with some added ingredient to make it more memorable. Here are several suggestions:

▪ Let each child decorate a plain brown shopping bag and create a Turn-Off Book Bag for carrying home the library books.

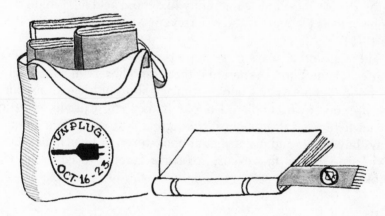

▪ Make homemade bookmarks decorated with the Turn-Off logo, or any other chosen design.

▪ Stop at an ice-cream store or bakery for a special treat on the way home.

▪ Include *all* members of the family—mother *and* father and all kids. This will inevitably emphasize the natural role that reading can play during a No-TV period—as the most logical and fulfilling replacement for TV watching.

At the library, take particular care to choose enticing reading material. This is not the time for parents to stock up on self-improvement books, or to finally launch into that long-deferred reading of Proust or *The Decline and Fall of the Roman Empire*. Nor is it the time for the kids to fill up their book bags with books relevant to their history or science project. Starting with the idea that for many kids the absence of television will be really hard—having something absorbing, and not too difficult, to read during those long hours can make a great difference. Books with good stories—mysteries, adventures, romances, science fiction—are what to look for, as well as "family fun" type books, with suggestions of games, projects, and activities that a family may do together.

While at the library, remember that the librarian is one of the natural allies of a TV Turn-Off and may be very helpful in recommending books and activities for your No-TV period. You might even get your local librarian thinking about the idea of a larger Turn-Off for the whole community like those held in Farmington, Connecticut; Piscataway, New Jersey; or Marshall, Missouri. (See part VI.)

There are other ways of setting up a stockpile of new reading matter for the Turn-Off period if there is no library in your neighborhood. Try borrowing books from neighbors or friends, or scouting up your own childhood books if they still exist in an attic somewhere. And if money isn't too great a problem, you can always buy books and magazines at bookstores, or by mail order. A TV Turn-Off is a fine excuse for some families to go on a real book-buying spree.

5. Picking a Reward

One of the most enjoyable pre-Turn-Off rituals is the special get-together to decide on a reward celebrating the end of the difficult experiment. The reward should be both appealing and appropriate—that is, something that would lead to greater family togetherness, and less TV viewing. A family trip everyone would enjoy—to an amusement park, for instance—is a good choice for a reward. The purchase of a special game or toy is another good choice. A special privilege, a special meal, better desserts for a month—all these make good rewards.

PREPARING THE TURN-OFF ACCESSORIES

1. The No-TV Button

All kids love wearing special buttons or badges. Having a No-TV button to wear during the Turn-Off may play a disproportionately important part in changing a child's attitude toward the experiment from hostile to enthusiastic.

If you can borrow or buy a button-making machine (see page 173 for ordering instructions), then all family members can make their own designs, ending up with a professional-looking button to wear during the No-TV period. Or you may buy ready-made buttons of TV stars and convert them into No-TV buttons by drawing a diagonal slash across them with an indelible marker. For younger children a simple button made out of cardboard and a safety pin and decorated with the No-TV logo or a design of their own choosing is probably as satisfying as one that is ready-made.

2. The Turn-Off Diary

For parents and kids old enough to do so, keeping a Turn-Off Diary with notes on how the absence of TV has changed daily life, and what alternative activities have taken its place, together with any thoughts, feelings, comments, and miscellaneous observations about the Turn-Off, is a most important part of the experiment.

The diary takes on greater importance if a certain effort is made in its preparation before the Turn-Off. It will make a real difference in the children's attitude toward the diary—and the Turn-Off itself—if a special cover is prepared, and if care is taken in the organization and design of the inside pages. See "The Turn-Off Diary" in the Appendix, page 173, for specific suggestions about the Turn-Off diary.

·5·

Go!
"Cold Turkey" and After

THE KICK-OFF CEREMONY

If the Turn-Off is to be something more than life-as-usual-with-one-thing-missing, it must start off with a bang. For this reason the "Kick-Off Ceremony," the final ritual before the Turn-Off begins, is especially important. It defines the actual beginning of the experiment, and establishes both the seriousness and the lightheartedness of the Turn-Off as a family project.

The best time for the Kick-off Ceremony is on the night before the Turn-Off begins, after the last programs have been watched. You may follow the step-by-step plan for a family Kick-off Ceremony on page 176. Or better yet, make up a ceremony of your own. After the Kick-off Ceremony, the diaries and No-TV buttons are distributed to every family member. The Turn-Off has officially begun!

HELPFUL HINTS FOR TURN-OFF SURVIVAL

Most families, even those who don't watch a great deal of television, are suprised to find that a week without TV presents unforeseen difficulties. Parents are often unaware of just how dependent they really are on television during certain times of the day—to fill time, to help them relax, to solve certain problems or defer the solving of other problems—and, of course, to provide periods of peace and quiet from the children.

Kids, too, rarely recognize how heavily time can hang on their hands without television to turn on when there's "nothing to do." These discoveries, of course, are the very reason a Turn-Off is so valuable. However, if the experiment is to be an effective instrument of change, it is most important that nobody in the family has a terrible time.

The "Turn-Off Survival Hints for Families," on page 160, offers a compendium of advice and concrete suggestions that will help you organize your family's time during the Turn-Off.

WHAT ABOUT THE VCR DURING A TURN-OFF?

During the planning stages of every Turn-Off a certain number of parents and a great number of children bring up the question of VCRs during the No-TV period. Does watching a movie or a pretaped program on the VCR constitute TV watching? The answer to this question is a very simple yes. While there are, indeed, advantages provided by the new technology of the VCR—better programs to be watched and a new freedom from the tyranny of TV scheduling that allows a family to have a leisurely dinner without missing out on a favorite program—nevertheless, for the purpose of a TV Turn-Off, watching a program on a VCR is still watching television. The idea of a No-TV Experiment is to expand a family's repertory of activities by allowing new free-time patterns to develop; making an exception for VCR programs would undermine this goal.

Families also ask (and again, especially the kids) whether it's all right to use a VCR to tape favorite programs during the Turn-Off for post-Turn-Off viewing. My answer is no. Taping programs would change the meaning of the Turn-Off. Instead of being a "No-TV Experiment" it becomes a mere "deferred TV" occurrence. The knowledge that every TV program is simply being put off until a later time rather than actually being replaced by different activities will subtly change the attitudes of all participants in the Turn-Off. The presence of television will still be powerful even during the Turn-Off, if the VCR is taking everything down on videocasettes for future consumption.

This is not to say, however, that an exception or two cannot be made if a special circumstance arises. (One special circumstance that may very possibly occur during a large-scale Turn-Off is coverage of the Turn-Off itself on the evening news. A VCR will come in very handy for such a situation.)

WHAT ABOUT VIDEO GAMES DURING A TURN-OFF?

If the purpose of a TV Turn-Off is to encourage new family activities, to give a view of what life was like before there was TV, and to encourage less passive activities such as reading, then it is far better to eliminate video games along with television programs. Besides, many families find it easier to actually remove their TVs or at least cover them up with a cloth or spread as a reminder that a Turn-Off is in progress; therefore, it would be difficult to reactivate the set for a video-game player.

THE FINAL PARTY

The successful completion of a TV Turn-Off, like the end of any other difficult and worthy project, deserves a ceremonial celebration. But unlike the Kick-off Ceremony focusing on the television set itself and the turn-off knob in particular, the end-of-the-Turn-Off celebration should definitely *not* include a ceremonial clicking on of the TV set. In fact, to avoid the very possibility of such an act, the final party should be considered an official part of the Turn-Off, whether it actually takes place during the established weeklong Turn-Off limits, or has to be held at a later time due to family members' scheduling difficulties.

Why not celebrate the resumption of TV viewing? For one thing, with habitual viewing patterns shaken up by a week's abstinence, it is quite possible that at the end of the No-TV period nobody will be thinking that much about television—at least for a while. That's great and is not to be discouraged by planning a "Turn-on" ceremony at the end of the Turn-Off. Besides, the purpose of the celebration is to applaud the gains of the No-TV Week—the increased family activity, the renewed interests in reading, hobbies, musical instruments, etc.—rather than to announce, even symbolically, that the family is going to resume its old patterns. The final party, therefore, might be a special meal—a picnic, an outing to a restaurant, or a dinner at home—and the celebration with its ritual accompaniments, clinking of glasses, toasts, speeches, and so on, should center on the successful conclusion of a difficult but gratifying experience, rather than a grateful return to the passive joys of TV viewing. The final party could also include readings from the Turn-Off diaries by parents and children.

■ EVERYTHING YOU NEED ■ FOR A FAMILY TURN-OFF

The two-part appendix at the end of this book provides practical help for families embarking on a TV Turn-Off. The first part, The Turn-Off Survival Kit, includes psychological support, if you need it, in the form of a summary of television's negative effects on children and families, and quotes from parents and children who have benefited from their Turn-Off experiences, as well as lists of activities families can do in place of TV viewing, and even some great recipes for home art projects. The second part, Nuts and Bolts, provides all the charts and forms, model contracts, and instructions for all the rituals and activities recommended for a Family Turn-Off. A step-by-step Checklist for a Family TV Turn-Off follows, with references to pages in the appendix.

Step-by-Step Checklist for a Family TV Turn-Off

1. Present and sell the idea to other family members. (See Survival Kit, page 153 to 166.)

2. Decide on date, at least two weeks in the future.

3. Order or make No-TV buttons. (See page 173.)

4. Have everyone sign Turn-Off contracts. (See page 174 or 175.)

5. Keep track of regular viewing on Family Viewing Chart during week preceding Turn-Off. (See page 168.)

6. During week preceding Turn-Off, take trip to library or bookstore and stock up on reading matter.

7. Make or buy Turn-Off diaries and decorate covers. (See page 173.)

8. All family members discuss and agree on reward.

9. Have a Battle Plan session, and fill in detailed battle plan for each family member. (See pages 169 and 170.) Include social plans for the Turn-Off Week, and plan to stock up on art equipment, games, etc. (See Turn-Off Survival Hints for Families on page 160, Letter to Kids Taking Part in a TV Turn-Off on page 171, and Basic Art Recipes, page 164.)

10. On the night before the Turn-Off, hold a formal Kick-off Ceremony. (See page 176.) Distribute diaries and No-TV buttons.

11. Have a party to celebrate the successful completion of your TV Turn-Off.

·6·
═══

How *Not* to Do
a Family TV Turn-Off

"It started, as it does with so many small children, with 'Sesame Street,' " says Tom Valeo, a reporter on the *Daily Herald* of Arlington, Illinois. "Soon my daughter was watching 'Mr. Rogers' and introducing her younger sister to the habit. Under the influence of the older kids in the neighborhood, they developed a taste for 'The Flintstones,' 'Popeye,' and Saturday morning cartoons. 'Sesame Street' was too tame for them; they needed stronger stuff. Then they discovered reruns of 'Three's Company.' . . . When they moved on to 'Taxi,' 'Happy Days,' and 'Diff'rent Strokes,' I knew things were out of hand. On top of that, they had a little brother toddling around, and he was getting hooked too. Drastic measures were needed. . . ."

So begins the terrible saga of a two-week Family Turn-Off Valeo initiated and subsequently wrote up as a fine feature story in his newspaper.[6] While the Valeos' Turn-Off was not a happy experience for them, as Tom Valeo's painfully honest narrative reveals, their experience clearly demonstrates that a successful TV Turn-Off involves more than simply unplugging the television set. In many ways the Valeo story serves as a cautionary tale of how *not* to do a Family Turn-Off.

Valeo begins his narrative by explaining the source of his anxiety about television: a haunting suspicion that excessive television viewing during his childhood had "damaged [his] mind." Here is how he came to that conclusion:

"I read a lot, but I wouldn't say I like to read. I like to find out about things so I read, but the act of reading is a lot of work for me. My wife, however, can spend hours lost in a good novel. . . . for her, reading is easy, rewarding, and fun."

He ascribes this difference to their childhood experiences with TV: "I never knew a time without TV," he explains. "I learned to read on schedule, and I always read well, but reading was never as easy or exciting as watching those flickering images on the TV screen. My wife, on the other hand, watched little TV as a child. Her parents had a TV but they didn't let their children watch it much. Consequently, my wife spent hours as a child curled up in a chair with a book, and she learned how to read for pleasure, a skill that still eludes me."

With these and other anxieties about television's effects in mind, Valeo proposed an experiment to his wife—"two weeks without TV, just to see what happens."

He elaborated on his fantasy of family life without television: of "our children playing together, drawing, using their toys and blossoming under the extra attention they'd get from us," and felt confident that his book-loving, TV-undamaged wife would welcome the idea of a Turn-Off. "We knew we were using TV as a baby-sitter and we both felt guilty about it," he explains.

His wife was unexpectedly cool to the proposal. "I'm the one who's going to bear the brunt of this," she observed. "Let's see you try to make dinner without the TV on."

Valeo prevailed. "Pulling the plug seemed the only right thing to do," he says. And pull the plug they did, with no particular plan of action and no prior preparation.

"The first thing I noticed was that all three of the kids were eating breakfast with me," Valeo writes as he describes the first day of the experiment. "That's wonderful, I thought, until I realized it meant the end of my morning meditation with the newspaper.

"My wife also found herself doing more things with the children," Valeo continues, although "there were moments when she was tempted to turn on the TV, just to keep them occupied while she unpacked the groceries or carried laundry downstairs, but she resisted.

"The first weekend was brutal," reports Valeo. "In the absence of television, it is very difficult to keep three children occupied from sunup to sundown. We were desperate for relief. A note I made on the first Saturday captures the ambiance of the household: 'I'm so exhausted I could vomit. . . . Toys are being scattered faster than I can pick them up.'

"Without the TV my wife and I became butlers responsible for fetching, playing, and answering questions all day. Instead of watching TV, the six-year-old was drawing, the three-year-old was painting her nails, and the toddler was climbing furniture all the time. The teasing and arguing among them was almost incessant, and the competition for our attention was becoming ferocious.

"So it went for nearly two weeks, until we left for vacation. When we returned, we were tired from the hectic trip and desperate for a little peace. We stumbled through the door, hoping to rest for a few minutes, but the toddler was raring to go. We took the easy way out—'Let's go see if "Sesame Street" is on.' It was, and the TV was back.

"I'm ashamed to admit it," Tom Valeo concludes in his article, "but the TV is on in our house just as much as before. What's worse, we have a VCR too. . . ."

What went so terribly wrong with the Valeo Turn-Off?

It is clear that the Valeos had been using television as a survival strategy from the time their children were infants, and were now deeply dependent upon it for child-care relief. As a result, without the sedative action of television to keep them in hand the little Valeos were not easy to manage—in fact, their uncontrolled behavior was enough to drive their poor parents to distraction ("I'm so exhausted I could vomit. . . .").

Perhaps if the Turn-Off had allowed the Valeos to come to the important realization that their children were so hard to manage without the help of television precisely *because* television had allowed them to grow up without some important behavioral controls, they might have set about establishing a different relationship with their children.

And yet, what if the TV *did* help the Valeos keep the kids in hand? Why not use any help they could possibly get during the trying years of parenthood? The answer is that a few years from then they might have a grave price to pay for taking the easy out: the unsocialized little children might metamorphose into uncontrollable older ones, bent on risk-seeking activities of a dangerous kind. It would be a bit late for child training, and television would no longer serve the purpose of keeping the kids under control. Nothing would.

Instead of coming to this understanding, however, the Valeos went back to their former television-dependent life. Tom Valeo ruefully reflects on this decision:

"In the diary I kept during the experiment is a line that startles me with its conviction," Valeo writes: " 'I'm clearly interacting more with the kids. I'm convinced that television is one of the most divisive influences on our family.'

"I still believe that," Valeo concludes. "We were much better off without TV, but I also know we'll never be without it again. I still feel guilty when I see the kids watching the same videotape again and again, but it's just so much easier to let them watch. I know they'd be better off without a TV in the house, but I don't think I could handle all the togetherness."

Underlying that resigned conclusion is the assumption that without TV life would always be the same nightmarish, chaotic mess that the Valeos endured during their two-week Turn-Off: the children would continue to be resentful and demanding, and the parents would forever be forced to take the roles of butlers, maids, and entertainers.

But Mrs. Valeo has only to look back at her own TV-less childhood to see that parents *can* survive perfectly well without using television for relief, or to look back just a little further at generations and generations of families before 1950 who managed to cook dinner, unload their groceries, and live a normal life without being driven crazy by their uncontrolled children.

It's not hard to understand why the Valeos went back to television with such alacrity: their Turn-Off experience had been an ordeal. All the fine ideas about television's baneful effects on children and families went down the drain in the awful reality of those two weeks.

Could the Valeos have managed their Turn-Off differently? Surely there are many other families today who are as dependent on television as a child minder as the Valeos. Can such families undertake a TV Turn-Off in a way that will be less disastrous than the Valeos'? The answer is an emphatic yes.

The difference between disaster and success lies in strategic preparation and planning—the sort of preparation that is detailed in this book. Without it, a Family Turn-Off takes on the chaotic, disorganized, and thoroughly miserable aspect so poignantly described in Tom Valeo's report. The difference also lies in an unambivalent commitment to family life.

What did the Valeos do wrong, and what might they have done instead to make their experiment successful?

• *They didn't "sell" the Turn-Off to the kids:* While two of the Valeo children were too young to be involved in family decision-making, the six-year-old was naturally resentful at having this "experiment" foisted on him and inevitably passed this resentment along to his younger siblings. Surely some of the children's wild and demanding behavior during the Turn-Off was based on their desire to sabotage this hateful project.

If the older child had been involved in the decision to try a TV Turn-Off in the first place, if it had been presented as a scientific experiment, if there had been a few amusing rituals connected with it, if there had been a reward waiting for everyone at the end—all the kids might have behaved quite differently during their two weeks without TV.

• *Poor timing:* A family vacation is not the best time for a Turn-Off. Parents have no escape from the kids (as they might when they go to work, for instance), and there are no familiar routines to take refuge in.

• *They expected miracles:* It is more than unrealistic for a family as dependent on television as the Valeos to simply unplug their sets for two weeks without any special planning or preparation and expect that some wonderful things will miraculously appear to fill in the vacuum—it is foolhardy.

It takes time to establish those play patterns and parent-child relationships that allow a family to live together in peace and harmony and allow the children to play on their own successfully without television. The Valeos expected miracles to happen instead of setting up things in advance to make their transition an easier one.

• *Inadequate advance planning:* If the Valeos had understood that they all needed support and help as they made a transition from heavy dependence on TV to "cold turkey," they might have made some plans for their two weeks without television, perhaps scheduling some social activities, inviting another family over for a meal, planning an amusing day trip, or at least borrowing a great supply of books from the library, including a book with some new family games or pastimes to fill time during the No-TV period.

• *Ambivalence:* Tom Valeo longed for a better family life and believed that "television is one of the most divisive influences on our family." And yet he deeply regretted losing his time alone with the newspaper when all three kids joined him at breakfast on the first day of the Turn-Off.

He dreamed of having more resourceful children who would be capable of "playing together, drawing, using their toys," instead of being hooked on television to fill their empty time. Yet he writes in his catalog of grievances: "Instead of watching TV, the six-year-old was drawing, the three-year-old was painting her nails, and the toddler was climbing furniture," and adds "dinners were particularly hectic because the kids would hang around after they finished and talk instead of dashing off to watch TV."

Nail-polish painting is perhaps not the most desirable activity for a three-year-old, but climbing furniture is certainly an honorable toddler pastime, and drawing is a perfect occupation for a six-year-old. Having the kids hang around at breakfast and after dinner, wanting to talk rather than watch TV is a dream of a fine family life.

Is it possible that the Valeos were somewhat ambivalent about the success of their TV Turn-Off? Without coming to understand that being a good parent calls for the development of some new abilities, among them being able to find more pleasure in talking to a noisy bunch of kids at breakfast than in reading a newspaper in peace and quiet, Tom Valeo cannot in fairness accuse television of being a "divisive influence." His own divided feelings about being a parent and having a family must be resolved before he can deal with the problem of television.

THE FAMILY CIRCUS

By Bil Keane

TEN GREAT EXCUSES FOR *WATCHING* TELEVISION DURING A TURN-OFF
(from Actual Kids' Diaries)

1. On Tuesday I went to my uncle's house but I forgot my No-TV button so I had to watch an hour of TV.

2. When I came home from school I found the lock of the door broken because my sister broke it by mistake. I was so nervous that I turned on the TV. When I am nervous I have to watch TV.

3. Friday: I went to my friend's house and my friend said she wanted to watch TV and it was her house so I didn't have a choice.

4. On Monday I watched some cartoons because I forgot that that day was the day we couldn't watch TV.

5. Dear Diary: In the morning I quit the Turn-Off and watched TV until 11 o'clock. Then I started again.

6. At lunch I made a big mistake. I watched a half hour of television. I promised myself if I did that again I'd take a switch and wack myself!

7. Today I felt bad because I couldn't watch the programs I love, so I took a little peek.

8. Dear Diary: I couldn't stand it so I watched 20 seconds of TV.

9. Well, I must confess I watched about 5 minutes of the Yankee game last night. My brother turned it on and the Yankees were close to scoring and I just *had* to watch.

10. Today my temptation burst. So I had to see "Wildside."

· Part III ·

The Classroom TV Turn-Off
(Grades 3 to 6)

You're an elementary school teacher with a keen respect for the importance of your mission: to educate, inspire, and perhaps permanently change the lives of those incompletely formed human beings in your charge—works in progress, you might call them. You have a classroom of children you deeply care about, sometimes worry about as well. And one of the things you worry about is television.

You know that some of the kids in your classroom watch too much TV and you worry about how it affects their work in school, their homework, even their physical condition in class. (How many times has a child fallen asleep in your classroom?) Some of the brightest, most capable children seem to be performing under par—bringing in sloppy assignments, being inattentive. Kids who seem naturally good readers don't seem to be particularly interested in books. You've noticed that if you present something complicated to a class, something that requires sustained concentration, a good number of kids seem to click you off, as if they were switching to a different channel. Could all those hours and hours of television viewing be having an adverse effect? You wonder if there's anything you could do . . .

WHAT IS A CLASSROOM TURN-OFF?

A Classroom Turn-Off is a group No-TV experiment initiated by a teacher for a class of children. The Turn-Off includes a number of activities and group rituals that help to transform it from a deprivation to a shared adventure and a challenge for the children involved. It also includes special classroom projects and assignments designed to cast light on television's role in children's and families' lives.

Any interested teacher can organize a successful Classroom Turn-Off as a class project. Its organization and planning do not require a great outlay of time and effort, yet the results may be as satisfying for its participants as those of more ambitious projects involving the whole school or community. Indeed, as the class involved in the Classroom Turn-Off begins to attract a certain amount of schoolwide attention, thanks to the No-TV buttons, diaries, and other rituals connected with the project, and as other families and teachers in the school begin to catch wind of some of the desirable social and educational consequences of the Turn-Off, the Classroom Turn-Off may well prove to be the first big step in the organization of a subsequent All-School Turn-Off.

Most of the plans and activities in this section are best suited to the middle grades of elementary school—grades three through six. Such "middle-aged" kids are old enough to enjoy the challenge of a Turn-Off and they are the perfect age to enjoy rituals such as the Kick-off Ceremony, the Contract, the Battle Plan. They are also eminently ready to get involved with hobbies, collections, and other new activities that might turn into lifetime interests . . . if only the right seed is planted at the right time. The Turn-Off is an opportunity to plant a few seeds.

Some families, of course, will "take the pledge" along with their children. But 9–12-year-olds are old enough to participate in a Classroom Turn-Off on their own, even to enjoy the drama and pathos of "going it alone" against the tantalizing backdrop of their parents' and siblings' regular programs.

·7·

Get Ready: Planning and Selling The Classroom Turn-Off

SEVEN GOOD THINGS
ABOUT A CLASSROOM TURN-OFF

1. Some kids will test their willpower during a TV Turn-Off:

Dear Diary:
Right now my brothers are watching my favorite pro-
gram and I am dying to watch it. It's 9:30 and I've been
through the day without TV. But the day isn't over yet. I
am so tempted to turn on the TV. I'm going for it! No, I
must stop. I must not turn it on! I'm not going to turn it
on. Well, Bye!
—Sixth grader, P.S. 84, New York City, No-TV Week

2. Some kids will start to think about television's effects on their lives during a Turn-Off:

When I heard our class wouldn't watch TV for a week
I thought it was dumb. Then I thought it was a good
idea, because I knew I was watching too much.
—Fifth grader, P.S. 166, New York City, No-TV Week

3. Some kids will gain new self-confidence from meeting the Turn-Off challenge successfully:

Dear Diary:
I had such a good weekend. Plus I did a lot of things

more interesting than watching TV. It made me feel happy for doing a hard thing by not seeing TV.
—Sixth grader, bilingual class, P.S. 84, New York City,
No-TV Week

4. Some kids will develop new interests that will color their lives long after the experiment has ended:

The week I turned off my television I read more books, my school work was better. I practiced piano more, I also learned to knit.
—Sixth grader, Richmond, Indiana, Turn-Off

5. For some teachers, the Turn-Off will provide new evidence of television's negative influence on school achievement.

Dear Diary:
When my mother came home this afternoon and she saw me doing my homework she said she couldn't believe it, because I always do my homework real late. Then I went to the store and saw Jimmy. Then I came home and started to read Confessions of a Teenage Baboon.
—Fifth grader, P.S. 84, New York City, No-TV Week

6. Other teachers will find out for the first time which children in their class are most affected by excessive TV viewing (the heaviest viewers on the pre-Turn-Off viewing chart often turn out to be the poorest achievers) and which children, consequently, need encouragement (either directly, or via their parents) to reduce their TV intake.

When I come home I CANNOT STAND IT. I want to turn on the TV set. When we didn't have No-TV week I always turned on the TV set and watched TV while I was doing my homework. That's why I always get some wrong on my homework. But now I only got two wrong. BUT I STILL CANNOT STAND IT!
—Fifth grader, P.S. 84, New York City, No-TV Week

7. For the class as a whole, the Turn-Off promises to lead to a new spirit of class solidarity, a shared sense of having been through something together that they will not easily forget.

PICKING A DATE

One thing Farmington learned in its TV Turn-Off campaign last year was that cooperation improved once the New Year's Day football blitz was over. So it is starting this year's effort a day later.

—The Hartford Courant

Having an actual date selected for the Turn-Off will make the experiment seem more real and official when you begin to discuss it with your class. Pick a date at least a month in advance, to give you a chance to set up a parents' meeting, to make or order accessories such as the No-TV button, and simply to give time for the idea to begin to roll and gain momentum among the children in your class and their families, and perhaps in your whole school community.

Guidelines on when *not* to schedule a Classroom Turn-Off:
- the week before or after a vacation
- the week of some much-heralded TV program
- the week of any class trip or planned event

SELLING THE IDEA TO YOUR CLASS

Getting everyone in the class to participate in your Classroom Turn-Off can be tricky. On the one hand, participation must be voluntary; the actual business of the project—not watching TV for a week—cannot be forced on kids and must, indeed, be gone into willingly and enthusiastically if the purpose of the Turn-Off is to be accomplished. On the other hand, only if the whole class takes part does it become a real event—one of those landmark experiences that bring a class together.

How are you to induce 100 percent of your class to voluntarily join the Turn-Off? The answer is that while participation in a Classroom Turn-Off must be voluntary, that does not mean that you as the classroom teacher cannot bring a certain amount of moral pressure to bear on your students. You believe in the Turn-Off—push for it! Also, you must present the idea to the kids in a way that will not scare them off.

In addition to the specific suggestions on page 159 for "selling" a TV Turn-Off to school-age children, here are some guidelines for presenting a Classroom Turn-Off in a persuasive way:

1. Strategic Timing

Present the idea of a TV Turn-Off to the kids in your class before you introduce it to anyone else. If they hear about it from a parent first, for instance, they are far more likely to reject it out of hand. If they see it as a special project the class will be doing, a "grown-up" sort of thing, not something "good for them" that adults always seem to be trying to impose, they are far more likely to join with enthusiasm, and perhaps even look forward to imposing it on their unwilling families!

2. Clarity and Confidence

Make your goal of 100 percent class participation perfectly clear. Tell the children that you consider it important for the whole class to do the Turn-Off together, that you *expect* them to take part, that you believe it will be a positive experience for everyone even if it sounds hard, and that you are confident that they will all participate.

3. TV Is Addictive

Using a bit of child psychology, emphasize to your class that TV viewing may be an addiction, at least for some viewers, and that quitting for a week may be really hard, like quitting smoking is for a smoker. The idea that the familiar act of TV viewing may actually be an addiction rarely fails to make kids interested in investigating this idea further. It also happens to be true:

> I find it very hard to resist my TV. It seems to stare at me, saying "Watch me. watch me, it's fun and relaxing!" But so far I've resisted it. The TV makes you want to watch it. You can get addicted without even knowing it. No-TV Week is so hard!
>
> —Sixth grader, P.S. 84, New York City, No-TV Week

4. No Penalties

Finally, make it clear that even though a serious effort to shut off the TV is required during the Turn-Off there will be absolutely no penalty imposed on anyone who gives in and does watch TV in a weak moment. Assure the children that all participants will still get the button and the diary, and be part of all the Turn-Off rituals, whether they manage to go "cold turkey" or simply cut down on TV viewing as much as they can.

Under these conditions it is not unlikely that all children in the class will agree to participate, and simply *try* to do their best. Even children who admit to "breaking down" and watching a considerable amount during a Turn-Off are inevitably reducing their usual TV intake considerably. As a sixth grader who watched a total of 4 hours of TV during a Turn-Off observed: "That's still 25 hours less than I usually watch during a week."

GAINING PARENTS' SUPPORT

My parents feel I watch too much TV. They think I'm always glued to it. Most of the programs I watch they hate except for educational stuff. Sometimes I wish my parents wouldn't watch TV because I am bored and I want to talk to someone. We do have rules that I should watch one hour of TV a day but I always watch more.
—Fifth grader, P.S. 84, New York City, No-TV Week

Involving as many class parents as possible in your Classroom Turn-Off will make a great difference to its success. Not only will the parents be more likely to offer needed help at occasions such as the final party, but their enthusiastic support will transmit itself indirectly into your classroom through their children: kids from participating families seem to throw themselves into the various Turn-Off activities with the most enthusiasm and inventiveness. Here are three steps to take to encourage maximum parent involvement:

1. A Parents' Meeting

Call a parents' meeting to discuss the Classroom Turn-Off two or three weeks before the planned event. (You'll find an organizational model for such a meeting on page 179.) It may not be easy to get a good turnout for this meeting—parents of "middle-aged" children are getting a bit middle-aged themselves, at least in their school spirit. But if you have done a good selling job in the classroom, the parents may have heard intriguing reports about the Turn-Off by now and be inspired to come and find out more. Sometimes kids whose class is planning a Classroom Turn-Off actually *make* their parents go to a meeting and then coax them to join the experiment—an amazing reversal after years of squabbling about television.

2. A Follow-up Letter

Since attendance at the parents' meeting will almost certainly not be 100 percent, you will want to send a letter to all parents, informing them about the forthcoming Classroom Turn-Off, explaining its purpose, and exhorting their cooperation, whether they choose to actually participate with their child or not. This letter should be distributed at least two weeks before the planned Turn-Off, to be taken home, and then returned with a parent's signature indicating whether the family plans to participate or not.

A model for such a follow-up letter appears on page 180. A Spanish translation is also included for schools with a bilingual population.

3. Turn-Off Survival Kits

As the actual Turn-Off approaches, the families of the children in your classroom may need some support, whether they are participating along with their child, or simply helping their child take part in the Turn-Off alone. Sending a special *Turn-Off Survival Kit* home with each child at the end of the pre-Turn-Off week is a strategic move at this point: it may actually help some parents make the decision to join the Turn-Off. It will also help those families for whom the Turn-Off will present a genuine challenge: not only to survive the week without TV, but to actively enjoy it. ("The Turn-Off Survival Kit" may be found in the appendix, from pages 153 to 166.)

THE TURN-OFF IS NOT JUST FOR KIDS

You mean we *would have to turn off too?*
—Teacher at staff meeting discussing a Turn-Off

Teachers, too, as it happens, have trouble with television, not only in its effects of the medium on the kids in their classroom, but also on them as parents and as marriage partners. Sometimes the trouble centers on their own habitual or even addictive viewing patterns.

It will make a great difference to the children in your class if you not only supervise their participation in the Turn-Off but also take an active part yourself. This means, first of all, making it clear to your class that you (and your whole family, if possible) are going to go "cold turkey" for the week along with them. It means taking part in the various rituals—signing the contract, wearing the button, keeping a detailed diary, and sharing your thoughts and difficulties.

Such direct teacher involvement inevitably leads to greater and more committed participation on the part of the class. "We're all in this together" is a powerful incentive for children to stick to their resolve not to give in to the pull of television during the Turn-Off. It may also make you begin to reconsider your use of TV as a classroom adjunct. Finally, it may make an unexpected difference in your own life as a private person and as a parent.

·8·

Get Set:
Special Rituals and
Preparations for the Classroom

MAKE IT AN ADVENTURE AND A CHALLENGE

Through the week I was in a lot of agony! With no TV I
almost died! But I made it through the week! It was even
kind of fun without the TV. . . .
—Third grader, Marshall, Missouri, Turn-Off

In the Classroom Turn-Off, everything depends on establishing
a positive attitude among the children involved. Only if the kids
develop a spirit of adventure and challenge about the experiment
will it allow them to open their lives to new and more fulfilling
experiences, and to begin to think about television in a new way.
The various preparations and rituals performed in the classroom
during the week before the Turn-Off play a most important role in
creating that spirit.

In general, although the rituals and preparations are similar to
those suggested for the Family Turn-Off, they become more fun in
a classroom situation. The participation of so many peers makes
the "survival" aspect of the Turn-Off especially enjoyable, akin to
an Outward Bound experience—something that may be hard but
will test the children's mettle in the company of their friends and
make them feel good about themselves afterward.

Remember, throughout the preparation period, that each specific step is intended to make the Turn-Off a special event, something important and out-of-the-ordinary. Make this your attitude
as a teacher as well. It is this extra dimension that will help compen-

sate for the real loss most regular TV viewers feel when they face a week without television.

CLASSROOM TURN-OFF RITUALS

1. The Contract

Signing an official Turn-Off contract, best of all one that somehow resembles an actual, legal and binding contract, is one of the rituals children respond to with the most enthusiasm. Not infrequently, students who have been undecided about whether to join a Turn-Off finally take the plunge at the very last minute when the official contracts are brought out for signing.

You may wish to use the sample contract on page 175, making copies for each participant in the class (and extras for participating families). Better yet, use it as a general model, but add a few special touches of your own relevant to your class and school. In all events, try to have a ribbon to attach, or a stick-on gold seal or, best of all, use a real seal, with sealing wax, to give the signing ceremony a very exciting touch.

The children should help in the preparation of the contract. You might start with a copy of the model contract on page 175, and then have each child do some fancy hand-lettering and other decorating to give it a special look. Or have all your students write their own version. The contracts are then collected and saved for the Kick-off Ceremony on the first day of the Turn-Off, when they are to be sealed with much seriousness and ceremony.

2. Pre-Turn-Off Viewing Charts

Now that my mom has seen my viewing written out she really doesn't like it.
—Fourth grader, P.S. 84, New York City, No-TV Week

During the week before the Turn-Off, ask all students in your class to keep a record of their regular home television viewing, using the "Family Viewing Chart" on page 168 or a chart of their own design that the kids can make in class. Encourage your class to keep this as carefully and completely as possible, emphasizing again that this information will provide important data in a scientific experiment. (Provide additional copies of the viewing chart for children whose whole family will be joining them in the Turn-Off.)

Since many parents are not completely aware of the extent of their child's television consumption, ask that each child return the chart each day with a parent's signature. For many parents, seeing the grand total of their children's daily viewing hours will be a revelation that may be the first step in gaining better television control.

For your purposes as a teacher, the viewing charts give an idea of who are the heavy viewers in the class. These kids will need the most support and help during the actual Turn-Off week. If these also turn out to be kids having trouble with schoolwork, this experiment can be useful in demonstrating to their parents the need for better TV control at home.

3. Class and Individual Battle Plans

For many children, time looms large when TV is unavailable. During pre-Turn-Off week, discuss the idea of empty time with the class and start the children thinking about alternative activities that can take the place of TV viewing during the Turn-Off. Begin by distributing the "Letter to Kids Taking Part in a TV Turn-Off" that appears on page 171. After going over the list with the class, encourage them to fill in the blank space with ideas for new activities.

Toward the end of the week, set aside time for students to work on their individual Battle Plans with specific ideas of how they will occupy free time during the Turn-Off week. (See page 169 for Battle Plan forms.) For those children being joined in the Turn-Off by their entire families, try to send home extra Battle Plan forms for the other family members.

Encourage the children to make group plans for the Turn-Off week by hanging an outsized page labeled "Class Battle Plan" in the front of the classroom. As the week goes on, fill it in with activities that either small groups of kids or the entire class plan to do during the Turn-Off week. These may include a weekend trip to the museum, or a Sunday baseball game and picnic, or an after-school trip to the public library to restock reading matter for the rest of the Turn-Off. The social opportunities offered by the Class Battle Plan, the new friendships that may form, or new adventures that may be undertaken purely in order to "fill" time are a gratifying side-benefit of every Classroom Turn-Off.

4. A Book Mountain

Just as television has dampened children's enthusiasm for reading, so, not surprisingly, the universal time-filler that takes the place of television during a Turn-Off is reading. From your vantage point as an educator, you will want to do everything you can to take advantage of this natural sequence of events and encourage children to read during the No-TV period.

The simplest and most effective way to get kids to read is to eliminate television and make available to them a great quantity of books. The Turn-Off will accomplish the first—you must encourage the second by means of book-stockpiling for each child during the week before the event.

Announce to the class that every child will need to accumulate a Book Mountain to help survive the Turn-Off. Let the children help you decide on an adequate number for the stockpile—ten, fifteen, twenty books. And then let each child proceed to accumulate books in a variety of ways until he or she has the requisite number stacked up somewhere in the classroom—ready to be read during the Turn-Off.

Where will the Book Mountain come from? The school library, first of all. The public library. From children's homes. From your own collection. Of course an effort should be made by the children to collect books that are appealing, that they really want to read. And emphasize to them that this is the occasion for the most engrossing, exciting, delightful books—books that will really make time go fast. Comic books? The children will like the idea of having them included, but specify a limited quantity—no more than one-quarter of the total stockpile can be comic books, magazines, or other sorts of non-books.

The stockpile remains in the classroom until the Turn-Off week. Then each child takes a certain number of books home every day, bringing them back to school when they are read to exchange for others.

But will the children be able to read so many books? What about those who have trouble reading, who hardly ever make it through even one book—why accumulate ten or fifteen for them? The answer is that the very idea of a Book Mountain is appealing. By making available such a large quantity for each child, you are increasing the odds that at least *some* of them will be read. In the end, you may be surprised at how many children will resort to voracious reading in the absence of television and make their way through to the very top of the mountain.

5. Planning the Class Reward or Party

> *Dear Diary, I am not going to watch TV for a week. Write now I would rather be watching TV. But I like doing this, aspashely because we are getting a party at the end of the week.*
> —Fourth grader, P.S. 166, New York City, No-TV
> Week

One of the most enjoyable tasks facing your class before the Turn-Off is deciding on a suitable reward for its successful completion. In reality, no reasonable reward is likely to compensate most children for the real loss they feel when they give up TV viewing for a week. Nevertheless, the very idea of a reward, and the opportunity to help decide what it will be, is psychologically important. Knowing that there will be a reward—any reward—makes the whole project appealing to kids from the start, though it is clear that the reward is not really why they are taking part in the Turn-Off.

What should the reward be? Some possibilities:

▪ *A desirable change in class routine:* a longer daily class read-aloud period for a month; a special class trip; one excused no-homework day.

▪ *A celebration:* a small party in the classroom with refreshments and time off from schoolwork; an out-of-school meal, or party, for the whole class. (The most thrilling location for such a get-together is probably your house. If that is not possible, then a parent might volunteer to be host for the party.)

PREPARING THE TURN-OFF ACCESSORIES

1. The No-TV Button

For a Classroom Turn-Off to succeed, a No-TV button for each child is an absolute necessity. It spreads word about the event most effectively. It makes kids who wear it feel special and important in the eyes of others. It imparts a sense of shared purpose to all participants.

The most important role of the button, however, may be symbolic: for contemporary kids, the promise of receiving something that is a standard and desirable part of "youth culture" allows them to suspend their natural resistance to a Turn-Off as well as the fear that if they go along with it they will be considered "nerds" by their peers. (See "The No-TV Button" on page 173 for more information about making and ordering buttons.)

2. The Turn-Off Diary

All children will be required to keep a daily diary during the No-TV period—an activity that serves both an educational and a psychological function.

Taking the time to decorate the diary in advance of the week may encourage the children to be more painstaking about their writing as well.

See page 173 of the Nuts and Bolts section for specific suggestions about the Turn-Off Diary.

CLASSROOM ACTIVITIES
AND ASSIGNMENTS RELATED TO TV

I thought No-TV week was a good experience. I learned there were a lot of other things I could do besides watch TV, even though once in a while I would kind of walk to the TV knowing it was No-TV Week and try to turn it on. But I never did. At those times I would feel very frustrated, but then I'd think It's only a week, so you SHOULDN'T *feel upset. Well, that's what I think. Bye!*

P.S. I haven't broken it yet, but I have a feeling I'm going to.
—Sixth grader, P.S. 84, New York City, No-TV Week

The week before the Turn-Off is a time to focus special attention on television, both in order to generate excitement about the forthcoming event and to take advantage of the educational opportunities that this unusual project provides. Some of these activities involve preparing materials the class will need for the Turn-Off—making the buttons, diaries, contracts, etc. Others are assignments that encourage kids to think about their relationship to television in a new way—not from the viewpoint of which programs they like and dislike but rather to help them consider how television affects their time, their schoolwork, their relationships. These assignments can range from simple descriptions of feelings about a TV Turn-Off to fanciful conversations about television with creatures from other planets. Two examples of children's writing before a TV Turn-Off follow:

Imaginary Conversation

"Beam! Buzz! Bonk! Clunk! Hel-lo—I am Bug-a-bug from Planet Dorf. How are you? I am here to find out about TV."

"Well, TV is a[n] entertaining fun thing to do, but people can get engrossed with it. It can overpower their lives so that they hardly do anything else."

"Are there other things to do besides watch TV?"

"Yes, of course, but many people don't do them because they are intranced by TV."

"Thank you, I must go now. Bye!"
—Sixth grader, P.S. 84, New York City, No-TV Week

Interview with Someone Who Grew Up before TV

> *I interviewed my grandmother. In her free time she
> would play with dolls, skip rope and read a lot. Her
> family activities were going to church, going to see plays,
> and visiting relatives. She does watch TV now, in fact a
> lot of TV. But she says she's glad she didn't have TV
> when she was little because she liked doing all the things
> she did.*
> —Fifth grader, P.S. 166, New York City, No-TV Week

On page 183 you will find a list of suggested activities, homework assignments, projects, and subjects for class discussion, many of them developed by teachers in Turn-Offs around the country.

Go!
"Cold Turkey" and After

THE KICK-OFF CEREMONY

On the morning of the first day of the actual TV Turn-Off, some children are likely to come into class all aflutter: they had completely forgotten about the Turn-Off and watched TV as usual before coming to school. Disaster! (And to think that you worried that the kids weren't going to take it seriously.) Reassure them that this does not "count," as it were, that the real Turn-Off is about to begin with the Kick-off Ceremony.

You may wish to follow the model Kick-off Ceremony on page 177. Or you and the kids may enjoy planning a different one, with special references that apply to your class alone. Your imaginations are the only limiting factor here. But keep in mind that this is the perfect occasion for drama, or better yet, melodrama. Do you have a quill pen? This is the perfect occasion to use it. Special background music during the ceremony—a funeral march, for instance—can help make the Kick-off memorable.

When the Kick-off Ceremony is over, everybody pins on a No-TV button. The Turn-Off has officially begun!

COLD FEET

Dear Diary:
I'm trying hard not to think about TV. Today after school I got home and straightened my room. Then I

watered the plants a little. Then I listened to the radio. Later I had dinner (It tasted disgusting), after dinner I did the laundry and planted some seeds. Then I started my homework and practiced the spelling a little. Then I printed some pictures with my brother. Then I wrote in my diary and now it's late and I'm EXHAUSTED *so I'm going to bed. Good night.*
—Fifth grader, P.S. 84, New York City, No-TV Week

Will the kids really do it? What's to keep them from simply watching all the TV they want, and *pretending* to be following the rules of the Turn-Off?

Skeptical outsiders often ask these questions when they hear about a Turn-Off. You may be suffering from an attack of cold feet about the experiment and secretly wondering the same thing yourself.

There's obviously no way to monitor what children do in the privacy of their homes. But if you have prepared for the Turn-Off in the right spirit of scientific inquiry, if you have emphasized the need for complete honesty in the diaries, and made it clear that there are no penalties for imperfect compliance of the Turn-Off rules, it's unlikely that the kids will cheat. It doesn't make psychological sense. The whole project would be no fun for them if they simply went home and watched as much as they usually do in the course of an ordinary week. As the Turn-Off progresses, you will have ample evidence in the kids' diaries, comments, and reactions to assuage any lingering doubts about their sincerity. For example:

I knew I shouldn't of signed that contract! Every time my mother turns on the TV I get temptive! I feel like saying "Forget it, who will know if I watch" but then I hold myself. Then I think I ain't going to hold myself any more. But I'll try and I know I will make it. What I mean is I'll try to make it through the whole week. I just watched 9 minutes of TV, but I won't watch any more!
—Sixth grader, P.S. 84, New York City, No-TV Week

THE TURN-OFF DIARY

Dear Diary: I feel like I'm dieing! I gotta watch TV! But I won't!
—Fourth grader, P.S. 166, New York City, No-TV
Week

Keeping a careful and accurate diary during the No-TV period is a most important part of the Classroom Turn-Off. Each participant's responsibility to record changes in daily life that may be connected with the absence of television underscores the Turn-Off's serious scientific purpose. This, in turn, helps compensate for the sense of loss and deprivation that so many regular TV viewers feel in its absence.

The diary also serves as a useful outlet for anxieties, and negative feelings about the experiment. It provides some literary-minded children with a forum for flowery and dramatic descriptions of their unique sufferings as they battle the *unspeakable* urge to turn on the television set.

If the class is unfamiliar with the concept of diary keeping, it might help to look at a few published collections of children's diaries to give them an idea of the various possiblities that keeping a diary provides. *Harriet the Spy,* by Louise Fitzhugh, is a children's classic that centers around a child who keeps a diary; if you plan sufficiently in advance, you might make this a read-aloud book in advance of the Turn-Off.

During the week of the Turn-Off allot a regular time each day to the Turn-Off diaries—preferably the first thing in the morning, when memory of yesterday's struggles (or triumphs) are freshest in the students' minds. Ask various children to read portions of their diaries aloud to the class. You might read excerpts from *your* Turn-Off diary as well.

You may gently encourage improved diary-keeping by pointing out and praising children's use of specific and vivid details in their entries, explaining the difference between such writing and generalizations. Also encourage honest descriptions of feelings, both positive and negative. It's better to avoid correcting these diaries for spelling or grammatical mistakes; they should be seen as spontaneous outlets, not as an assignment.

THE CLASS REWARD

Enjoy it, whatever it was that you all picked. You heartily deserve it! And don't keep it a secret from the rest of the school—the knowledge of your project well accomplished and well rewarded will serve to encourage others to try the Turn-Off idea in their own classrooms.

TURN-OFF FOLLOW-UPS

Shortly after the Turn-Off has ended, send all parents a questionnaire to gather information about their Turn-Off experiences. A model questionnaire appears on page 184.

A few weeks or a month after the Turn-Off, distribute new viewing charts to the children and ask them to keep records of their home TV viewing for one more week. You may be amazed to see that viewing hours will have declined significantly for many children in your class. (Once again, collect these with a parent's signature.)

The material you gather after your Turn-Off is valuable, and should be shared with others. Send a summary of parents' comments and comparative viewing statistics to your school principal to influence school attitudes about television and perhaps to help bring about policy changes on a school-wide basis. Discouraging TV viewing of any sort in the classroom itself is one desirable step a principal may take; suggesting that TV programs should not be assigned as homework is another.

You are also encouraged to send in summaries and personal observations about your Classroom Turn-Off to the address given on page 198, at the end of this book, for inclusion in future editions of *Unplugging the Plug-In Drug*. This information may help influence other teachers and parents throughout the country to give the TV Turn-Off idea a try.

■ EVERYTHING YOU NEED ■ FOR A CLASSROOM TURN-OFF

The appendix at the end of this book provides most of the actual materials you will need for your Classroom Turn-Off. The Turn-Off Survival Kit (pages 153 to 166) may be copied and distributed to all participating parents. In the Nuts and Bolts section you will find all the appropriate forms, charts, and letters, as well as detailed instructions for the rituals and ceremonies. The Step-by-Step Outline that follows will direct you to the exact pages where you may find the needed materials.

Step-by-Step Checklist
for a Classroom TV Turn-Off

1. Sell the Turn-Off idea to the kids in your classroom (page 159).
2. Together with kids, pick a date, and decide on reward or party.
3. Enlist parents' support for the Turn-Off through parents' meeting and follow-up letter to parents (page 180).
4. Send out Turn-Off Survival Kits to all class parents (pages 153 to 166).
5. Distribute Letter to Kids Taking Part in a Turn-Off (page 171).
6. Order or borrow button-making machine for No-TV buttons, or decide on substitute button (page 173).
7. Week before Turn-Off:
   a. Distribute viewing charts and collect each day, with parent's signature (page 168).
   b. Distribute Battle Plan forms, and work on them in class. Start a Class Battle Plan (page 169).
   c. Have kids help prepare contracts (page 175).
   d. Have kids help prepare and decorate diaries (page 173).
   e. Do classroom activities related to TV (page 183).
8. Hold Kick-off Ceremony on first morning of the Turn-Off:
   a. Follow ritual ceremony.
   b. Sign and seal contracts.
   c. Distribute diaries and No-TV buttons.
9. During Turn-Off Week, have daily readings from diaries.
10. Have final party, or take part in the planned reward.
11. Do follow-up studies:
    a. One week after Turn-Off, send questionnaire to all participating parents.
    b. One month after Turn-Off, follow up on one week's viewing and compare with pre-Turn-Off viewing statistics.

Part IV

The Early Childhood Turn-Off
(Nursery School, Kindergarten, Grades 1 and 2)

*During the Turn-Off I noticed a difference in the class.
The children were less tired, their play was less violent,
and they were better listeners.*
—Kindergarten teacher, Farmington, Connecticut,
Turn-Off

As a teacher of children in the early grades, you are well aware of television's negative impact. Not only do you see the effects of violent or crude programs on children's play (with cheap superheroes universally replacing traditional, archetypal figures in young children's make-believe play), but you have long been observing a greater passivity about play in general and a diminished ability to focus sustained attention on a given task among many of the children in your classroom, changes that seem more related to the particular experience of television viewing than to the specific contents of programs that appear on the screen.

You know that a large part of your job as teacher is not directed at children alone—you are an enormously important educator for young parents as well. Since family television patterns set during the early childhood years can decisively affect a child's educational future, you have a responsibility to educate parents about television and its negative potential.

An Early Childhood TV Turn-Off is a parent-education project well suited for this purpose. It is designed to shed light on the role television plays in child development, to show how it influences family life and child-rearing strategies, and to pave the way for better television control. Though organizing a Turn-Off for your class and gaining parents' support and cooperation will cost you some time and effort, the knowledge that you may have provided the children in your class and their parents with one of the most enlightening and far-reaching educational experiences they will ever have will be your reward.

WHAT IS AN EARLY CHILDHOOD TURN-OFF?

An Early Childhood Turn-Off is a group No-TV Experiment involving young children from nursery school through second grade and their families. While it is organized by a teacher for a classroom of children, nevertheless it requires a different plan from the Classroom Turn-Off outlined in part III of this book. This is because very young children have not yet acquired the skills needed to participate in the Classroom Turn-Off's various educational activities, nor can they make the decision to take part in a TV Turn-Off independently, without the cooperation of their whole families. Their parents must be the ones who decide to try a week without television and supervise a Turn-Off plan within their own family. But the fact that many families will be participating at the same time adds considerable excitement and fun to the event for parents and children both.

An Early Childhood Turn-Off presents an organizational challenge to the teacher in charge: first, to convince a group of parents not only that they can survive a week without television, but that it may be a turning point in their family life; then to provide materials, help, and encouragement to the parents involved in order that they may reap the greatest possible benefits from the experience.

This section provides guidance for teachers wishing to organize an Early Childhood Turn-Off, and several suggestions for simple classroom activities that are appropriate for young children. At home, however, the children and families involved in this Turn-Off will follow the basic plan for the Family Turn-Off as outlined in part II of this book.

10

Get Ready: Planning and Selling the Early Childhood Turn-Off

This Turn-Off seemed harder for the parents than for the children.

—Parent, Marshall, Missouri, Turn-Off

THE PARENTS' MEETING ABOUT TELEVISION

Selling the idea to your class parents and gaining their cooperation will not be an easy task. As parents of young children, they are far more likely to depend on television for relief from child-care burdens than parents of older kids and, understandably, more likely to panic at the idea of a week without television.

Holding a parents' meeting about television is the best way to introduce the idea of a Turn-Off to class parents and to reassure them that their survival is not jeopardized by turning off TV. Your own conviction about the importance of the subject is crucial—first in getting parents to attend the meeting and then in persuading them to give the Turn-Off a try. Here are a number of strategies to increase the likelihood of high attendance at a meeting about television:

1. Send out a persuasive notice a few weeks in advance of your planned meeting date, and then send out a follow-up notice.

2. Make sure parents receive and read the notice by requiring that they return it with a signature.

3. Arrange for child care during the meeting. Many parents will not attend if they have to pay for a baby-sitter.

PLANNING A PARENTS' MEETING

Quite a few parents are unenlightened about the negative impact of excessive television viewing, believing that their responsibility resides mainly in protecting their children from unsuitably violent or sexually explicit programs. The parents' meeting is an opportunity to raise consciousness about some of the ways television affects child development and family cohesiveness apart from program content. You may wish to follow the sample notice on page 178, and then follow the suggested outline for a meeting on page 179. At the end of the outline, you will find some guidelines for selling the Turn-Off idea effectively.

A FOLLOW-UP LETTER

Even if 100 percent of the parents in your class attend the meeting about television and sign on for the Turn-Off, a follow-up letter summarizing the purpose of the experiment and your belief in its value is strategically important: it will keep up interest in the project and help prevent cold feet from developing among those who have already volunteered to do it.

If (more likely) some parents do not attend, a follow-up letter gives you another chance to enlist support for the Turn-Off. Send this letter home with the children at the end of the school day at least two weeks before your chosen date, and ask that it be returned with a parent's signature indicating whether the family plans to participate.

A model follow-up letter may be found on page 181.

11

Get Set:
Classroom Rituals
and Preparations

Although the rituals that precede the Early Childhood Turn-Off are necessarily simpler than those suggested for older children, they are nevertheless crucial to the success of the experiment. The children gain a sense of being involved in something serious and important and come to see that the Turn-Off is an event in itself, not a mere turning off of their enjoyable television programs. Even preschoolers can come to understand, although simply, that watching television is a different sort of experience from actually doing things such as drawing, pasting, making collages, listening to a story, or talking to another person. (In reality, parents need this lesson more than their small children. Most little kids actually prefer real activities to TV viewing.)

THE CONTRACT

A contract-signing ceremony in the classroom a few days before the Turn-Off is a ritual all young children enjoy. It makes them feel grown-up and important, and besides, it gives them a clear idea of what exactly the Turn-Off is about. Distribute copies of the Early Childhood Contract on page 174 to the class, having filled in each child's name and the dates of the Turn-Off in the appropriate spaces. Or you may wish to design a different contract with your own wording. You may have the children decorate the contracts before the ceremony begins, perhaps drawing a colorful border around the margins, or making any other design of their choosing in the blank spaces.

As the ceremony begins, explain what a contract is—an agreement between two or more people, which is legal and binding—that is, a part of the law, and therefore cannot be broken. Tell them that if they sign the contract, they are saying that they will try their very very best to do what it says (assuring them, however, that nothing bad will happen to them if they cannot do exactly what the contract says—they just have to try.)

Now read aloud the words of the contract, perhaps to the background of some solemn music to give the ceremony a serious air. Then have each child come up, one by one, raise his or her right hand, and say: "I agree to keep the contract," and then have them sign at the bottom, either with their names, or with a simple X in the way of all preliterate folk. Collect the contracts for use in the Kick-off Ceremony, when a seal will be attached and the Turn-Off will officially begin.

THE TURN-OFF PROJECT

Before the No-TV Week, have each child pick one special project to work on during those times that might otherwise be spent watching TV. This may be chosen from any number of art projects, a list of which you will find beginning on page 164. If a child plays a musical instrument, the Turn-Off project might be to work on learning a piece on the piano, violin, accordion, or whatever. It may be a cooking project or a sewing or knitting project. If possible, the results of the child's work at home should be brought in to school after the Turn-Off.

THE TURN-OFF READ-ALOUD BOOK

Encouraging home reading aloud is one of the great goals of an Early Childhood Turn-Off. For this reason, a read-aloud ritual is planned as part of the official Turn-Off structure and written into the contract.

During the week before the Turn-Off each child is to help select one long or several short read-aloud books to take home for daily reading during the Turn-Off period. Parents, of course, are encouraged to help in the selection of these books.

In addition, for children who have already learned to read, make available as many good reading books as possible for taking home during the No-TV period, and whenever possible, encourage parents to make special trips to the library, as called for in the Family Turn-Off. For a fine list of tried and true Read-aloud books for all age groups, see Jim Trelease's *Read-Aloud Handbook*.

PREPARING THE TURN-OFF ACCESSORIES

1. The No-TV Button
All children involved in a TV Turn-Off of any sort enjoy wearing a special No-TV button during the actual event. While older children are likely to scorn anything but a commercial-looking button, children in the early childhood years gain more satisfaction from making their own out of heavy cardboard or oaktag.

For the youngest children, you may provide a circle of paper with the No-TV logo on it to color in their own way and then paste onto a circle of cardboard. First and second graders may choose to create their own designs, and make their buttons entirely themselves, using a compass or a small glass to get a perfect circle. The button is then attached to the child's clothes with a large safety pin. Of course, if you have access to a button-making machine, the children will enjoy making their own designs for "real" buttons too. (See page 173 for ordering a button-making machine.)

2. The No-TV Reminder Sign
Another good make-it-yourself project for young children is to design and construct a No-TV sign to be taped over all TV sets in the house as a reminder that a Turn-Off is in progress. Again, children may create their own designs, with suitable drawings of favorite TV programs, etc., or may simply copy the No-TV logo on a piece of paper. But each child should make as many of these signs as there are TV sets at home.

3. The No-TV Diary
Although children in an Early Childhood Turn-Off are too young to keep a real diary during the No-TV period, diary-keeping

is nevertheless an important part of the experiment as it will take place in their homes. Parents will be more likely to keep a diary if you provide one for the children to take home, especially a beautifully decorated one.

The diary may simply be seven pieces of paper stapled together and then attached to a cover appropriately decorated by each child.

More information about No-TV Diaries appears on page 173 of the appendix.

4. Viewing Charts

A week before the Turn-Off, give each child a viewing chart to take home, for keeping a record of pre-Turn-Off home viewing. Parents are far more likely to keep records if the actual chart is provided. You may use the model on page 168.

THE TURN-OFF SURVIVAL KIT

A Turn-Off kit for parents containing information and survival aids for the No-TV period may make a real difference—both in persuading parents to join the experiment, and in making the week, once it arrives, an easier and more enjoyable experience for the families involved. It may be handed out to parents at the parents' meeting about television, and sent home via the children to those who did not attend. The first part of the appendix of this book includes suggested pages to include in the Survival Kit.

·12·

Go!
The Turn-Off Week Itself:
Classroom Activities

After the TV Turn-Off week was over, Josh said, "Mommy, can we still have times when we turn the TV off? We had so much fun." And we've been doing just that.

—Parent, Buffalo Great TV Turn-Off

THE KICK-OFF CEREMONY

Here is a simple Kick-off Ceremony to get the Turn-Off started officially in your classroom. (The children and their families are encouraged to have their own home Kick-off Ceremony, either following instructions in their Turn-Off survival kits, or devising one of their own.)

The ceremony centers around a TV set—a real or make-believe TV made out of a cardboard carton decorated by the children, or one constructed out of building blocks.

1. With solemnity, cover up the TV set or facsimile with a blanket or sheet, explaining that the television set is going to sleep for a week, both in school and at everybody's home.

2. Continue with ritual farewells to TV watching. One by one, each child is invited to go up to the TV set, say good-bye, and then tell one thing he or she would like to do during Turn-Off week instead of watching TV.

3. Conclude the ceremony by attaching a gold seal (or facsimile) on each child's contract as a token that the contract is now binding.

4. Finally, distribute the No-TV buttons the children have prepared. The Turn-Off has officially begun!

CLASSROOM ACTIVITIES DURING THE TURN-OFF

1. Show and Tell

In the early grades, most classes have a time and place for getting together as a group and giving children a chance to talk about what's on their minds—Show and Tell is the most common name for this gathering. This is a natural time and place to discuss television and the children's reaction to its absence. Have the children report on what new activities are replacing TV watching in their families, and keep a list of them posted in the front of the classroom. Encourage children to bring in their family No-TV diaries so you can read excerpts to the class.

2. A TV Program in your head

When you read a story aloud to your class during the Turn-Off week, discuss with the class how listening to a story is different from watching a TV program. Explain the idea that when they listen to a story without pictures, they are actually creating their own television program in their heads.

3. Before TV . . .

Have a class discussion centering on how people spent their free time before there was television. Have children ask their parents and grandparents if they remember what life was like before everybody had a TV set at home.

CONSPICUOUS TEACHER PARTICIPATION

If at all possible, be sure that you are a conspicuous participant yourself in your class Turn-Off. Your own example is all-important as a model and reassurance to both parents and children in your class. Wear the button every day. Sign a contract. Keep a diary, and perhaps read excerpts from it to your class. If you have young children of your own, make a particular effort to tell your class of their experiences—this will serve as a particularly powerful source of inspiration.

THE FINAL PARTY

A final party after the Turn-Off, to celebrate the completion of the week without television and to go over what everyone has learned from the experience, is part of the deal as written in the contract. Invite parents to come if they can. Encourage the children to talk about the things they did at home that week, and what felt different about life without TV.

Of course a special treat—cupcakes or home-baked cookies provided by some dependable parent—is a crucial part of this celebration. A further sign of recognition—a special certificate of merit, for instance—can be handed out to each child who didn't watch TV all week. A small prize for each participant was also promised. You may be able to find some inexpensive token prize—and provide these yourself, or you may ask each parent to contribute an inexpensive gift to a grab bag and let each child draw from it during the party.

■ EVERYTHING YOU NEED FOR AN ■ EARLY CHILDHOOD TURN-OFF

Most of the matterials you'll need for carrying out an Early Childhood Turn-Off for your class are provided in the appendix at the end of this book. The following Step-by-Step Outline will refer you to the exact pages in the appendix or the previous text where you may find the necessary material to copy and send to parents, or instructions to follow for the various rituals and preparations.

Step-by-Step Checklist
for an Early Childhood Turn-Off

1. Hold a Parents' Meeting about television to sell the Turn-Off idea to parents (see page 179).
2. Send Follow-up Letter to Parents about Turn-Off (see page 181).
3. Turn-Off Rituals—in Classroom, the week before the Turn-Off begins:
    a. Contract (page 91)
    b. Turn-Off Project (page 92)
    c. Turn-Off Read-aloud book (page 92)
4. Prepare Turn-Off Accessories in classroom:
    a. No-TV Button (page 93)
    b. No-TV Reminder Sign (page 93)
    c. Family No-TV Diary (page 93)
    d. Viewing Charts (page 94)
5. Send Survival Kit to all parents with instructions for Family Turn-Off (pages 153 to 166).
6. Hold Kick-off Ceremony in classroom (page 95).
7. Activities during Turn-Off Week (page 96):
    a. Show and Tell about Family Turn-Off (page 96)
    b. Imagination exercises (page 96)
    c. How people spent free time before TV—discussion (page 96)
8. Final Party (page 97).
9. Follow-up Questionnaires (page 184) and Viewing Charts (page 168).

· 13 ·

Unable to Cope Without TV

Susan and Fred Craig, parents of one-year-old Kim, decided to participate in a TV Turn-Off not, as in most cases, because a child in the family watched too much TV but because of a parent's addiction problem.

"I use TV as a substitute for everything," Susan Craig admitted. She was worried about whether she would be able to cut down her TV consumption when she started law school in September. The diaries she kept of TV-related events for two weeks before the Turn-Off, and then during the No-TV period itself, reveal a painful struggle against a serious dependence on television, as well as a rare look at the actual transition of a young child from non-viewer into real viewer.

EXCERPTS FROM THE PRE-TURN-OFF DIARY:

July 9. I turned on the TV at 11 a.m.—it stayed on till 10 p.m., but I didn't watch continually. I use the sound for "company" while I clean house, fix meals, read, etc. Kim (age 1) watches short segments such as commercials, especially singing ones, usually as a break in other activities.

July 10. TV turned on at 12 noon for news. Turned off at 1:30 p.m. Turned on "Sesame Street" at 4 p.m. (first time ever) for Kim. She was fascinated for 10 minutes, then got off couch and played with toys.

July 11. TV turned on at 3 p.m. Kim watched part of "Sesame Street," but didn't pay much attention to it.

July 12. Kim wanted nothing to do with "Sesame Street" today so we watched reruns on Channel 2—she enjoys the introductions to "McHale's Navy" and "Bewitched."

July 13. I turned on TV at 10:30 a.m., watched soap operas. Kim reacts very favorably to certain characters. Set off at 12, on again at 5.

July 14 (Sat.). I turned on cartoons in a.m.—I enjoy them—Kim was intrigued by "Star Trek" (cartoon) but ignored such "modern" cartoons as "Butch Cassidy." Turned off at 12. On again at 4 with adult selections.

July 15. Fred and I watched mystery movies in the morning. Kim's interested in unusual noises coming from the set but nothing much else. Watched assorted films during day and evening.

EXCERPTS FROM DIARY DURING THE NO-TV PERIOD:

July 16. Managed to keep TV off till 4 p.m.—Kim started playing with dials so I turned it on—she watched part of "Sesame Street" and set remained on the rest of the evening.

Sun., July 17. Plenty of yard work and shopping to do so TV off until 4:30. Fred and I watched "Star Trek" reruns. Then he watched a mediocre movie. Both struck by Kim's growing attraction to TV. She will sit and stare at it for several minutes at a time with no awareness of anything else.

July 18. A day without TV although very tempted around 5 p.m. when Kim very cranky and irritating. But it stayed off until the 8 p.m. movie.

July 19. Another day without TV—no bad reactions from any of us.

July 20. I had a bad cold today and spent most of the day in bed. Fred and Kim watched TV most of the day.

July 21. Still recovering from cold—unable to cope with Kim's energy and demands. Turned TV on at 11:30 a.m. to give her something quiet to do. It didn't work. She ignored the TV and pestered me. Turned it off at 1 p.m. We both took naps. Turned it on again when Fred came home about 6:30 p.m.

July 22. No TV at all today.

July 23. Kept TV off until 4 p.m. Had to dry my hair and turned on "Sesame Street" to keep Kim busy. She was thrilled—danced and laughed during opening song and really watched the number sequences. Her attention span has increased greatly over the past few weeks. During evening after Kim went to sleep Fred watched a football game while I read magazines.

Sue's general notes at end of first week:

> I know the Turn-Off was a partial flop. I was able to keep it off sometimes during the day, but by 4 p.m., I was so tense and tired I turned it back on to give Kim and me something to do. Biggest factor was Kim—without the TV I find myself doing more things, housework, etc., and less likely to sit down. Kim however is used to having me available to play frequently and is upset by my new activity—so much so that she gets on my nerves by fussing about it. I am surprised by the discovery that my television viewing has affected her even if she doesn't watch. I'm going to keep trying, but with an emphasis on giving Kim some of my time and teaching her some independence too.
>
> What the Turn-Off taught me was that we all can live without it but it is necessary to plan some activities, especially in the early evening when household chores are done and boredom sets in. In the time since the Experiment I have eliminated all daytime watching—except "Sesame Street." Kim still watches. She gets such a kick out of it I don't have the heart to stop her watching. We have been able to cut down to 2 hours nightly except (1) on weekends, and now that football season is starting it will get worse; (2) days when I am exhausted or not feeling well and I use it as a tranquilizer for myself and a baby-sitter for Kim.
>
> The most important thing I noticed after we turned the set back on was Kim's reaction. She is now almost 15

months old and instead of occasional glances at the set she frequently sits right in front of it and watches. Her watching is really more of a stare—she gets glassy-eyed and remote. Since I find myself watching in the same way, I am struck by a similarity to drugs. The TV *does* seem to provide the same passive, total escape that drugs do.

Postscript: October 6. At this time I have been in law school for 3 weeks. I'm happy to say that I have no trouble turning off the set and studying—we do watch "Sesame Street" and the news. Have to credit the Turn-Off with making the transition easier by proving that it can be done.

Reading the Craig diary reveals a broad range of potential problems families may have in dealing with television. The parents in this family have problems with their own viewing—Sue Craig admits that she uses television as a relaxant, an avoidance mechanism, an escape from relationships. Television's negative impact on child-rearing is clear in this case history, as Sue recognizes that she has trouble coping with her child's natural energy and demands without using television as a tranquilizer for herself and, gradually, a baby-sitter for the child.

· Part V ·

The School
Turn-Off

A GREAT TURN-OFF IN MARSHALL, MISSOURI

Martha Thornton is a remarkable school librarian in Marshall, Missouri, who dreamed up, planned, organized, and ran the Marshall TV Turn-Off that took place March 6–13, 1986. I spoke to her shortly after the Turn-Off was over, and she told me how the project was put together and how it all worked. Her story, in her words, gives a good picture of what lies ahead for anyone planning to organize a School Turn-Off.

"I'm still in a bit of shock about the whole thing, how successful it was, and what huge participation we got. But of course we all did a lot of work on it beforehand, and that was important.

"The kids got revved up about it in school. First I presented it to them when their class came into the library—I tried to make it seem an adventure. Then their teachers talked to them about it in their classrooms. They accepted it because it was not something foisted on them by parents. In fact, many kids came home and said they were doing the Turn-Off no matter what and had to persuade their parents to go along. I think one reason the kids liked it was because they had more of their parents' attention for a whole week. The kids' reaction did amaze me—I thought we might get 500 tops, doing it under duress. Instead, we had 1,034 kids voluntarily signing pledge cards. That's about 75 percent of all our elementary school students. And 96 percent of the parents said they'd do it again if we had another Turn-Off next year!

"A hard task was explaining the purpose of the Turn-Off—this wasn't immediately understandable to a lot of people—the idea that excessive television watching might be affecting their lives and their kids' learning. But we had good publicity in the newspapers, which helped people understand what we were aiming at.

"Here's how we went about organizing the Turn-Off:

"I began in September when the four elementary schools in Marshall all have school open houses. I gave a little spiel about the Turn-Off idea at each of these, explaining some of my concerns about excessive viewing and its effects on children's school achievement and on family life. I broke the idea gradually to the parents and teachers at this point, telling them that we'd be doing a Turn-Off later on in the school year.

"The next step was talking it over with the principals of the schools. I can't say that they were particularly enthusiastic, but they said they would take part.

"Then, in November, I sent a letter out to all the teachers explaining the Turn-Off idea and asking for volunteers to work on the organizing committee. I had quite a response—about 20 teachers out of staff of 60 were enthusiastic about the idea. Many teachers spoke to me about their anxiety about TV's impact on learning.

"Maybe that enthusiastic reaction was why I was unprepared for what happened at the faculty meeting on February 4, a special meeting called for the purpose of discussing the Turn-Off. I expected the whole staff to be totally delighted with the Turn-Off idea—to be grateful to us for doing it. Instead, many people at that meeting were hostile and defensive. One teacher defended violence on television—there's violence in books too, she said. When I said that part of the Turn-Off meant no instructional TV during that week, no audiovisual aids to be used in the classroom, no filmstrips, no films, there was an audible gasp in the room. A lot of teachers are very dependent on these aids. I don't know where the enthusiastic teachers were during that meeting—they didn't speak up, somehow. But later, as the ball got rolling, most of the teachers did come round—even the most negative ones.

"Next thing, in January I went to the P.T.A. for support. They agreed to go along, and to give some financial support to the project. At this point I set up 3 committees: a 'pre-committee' for planning and organizing, a 'week-of committee' for projects going on during the Turn-Off, and a 'post-committee' for the party and follow-ups. These were committees of teachers and parents, about 4 on each committee.

"The 'pre-committee' began work: renting a Jim Trelease *Read-Aloud* film and organizing a showing; doing all the publicity for the Turn-Off, press releases to the papers, etc.; we got kids to sing jingles on radio: to the tune of "Row Row Row Your Boat," they sang Turn, Turn, Off TV; also kids did testimonials on the radio about what they were going to do instead of watching TV. The committee also organized programs at all the service clubs (Rotary, Kiwanis, Optimist, Lions) explaining the Turn-Off and getting their commitment and financial support.

"Another great thing the 'pre-committee' did was the Book Fair. Instead of trying to make money, they sold the books at the discount they bought them for, with the idea of getting people to buy as many books as possible. They sold $2,000 worth of books at the Fair!

"In mid-January, I went to the Board of Education and presented them with a resolution and asked them to back it—and to set aside the week of the Turn-Off as TV Awareness week. This was important because later on I'd have people asking if the Board of Education was behind this and I'd be able to say yes. Fortunately, the Superintendent of Schools had been to one of our open houses in September and had liked the idea then, and he backed it now. Later he sent a directive to all teachers telling them that he considered this educationally sound, that it would be good for our school district, and that he was behind it.

"By the middle of February the 'week-of committee' began to work—putting out calendars of activities people could do during the Turn-Off. We don't have a public library in Marshall, so we didn't have that resource. But we managed to set up quite a number of good things—story hours after school every day; a TV Hotline parents or kids could call for moral support or advice or just for help with homework. Some parents just called the Hotline to tell how nicely their children were playing together without the TV on!

"The main job of the 'post-committee' was Recognition Night. Marshall has a population of only 12,000, so the idea that 800 people came to the Recognition Night party is really amazing. Many kids did performances: there was the King Tut skit, about what Tut did when there was no TV; a poem by a fifth-grader with the refrain:

> Turn the TV off, it's not a sin,
> Turn the TV off, you're bound to win,
> Turn the TV off and you will see
> There's more to living than watching TV.

"The grand finale was called TV Busters—everybody loved it. Then some families gave testimonials about their experiences, and finally we had a drawing among the 75 'cold turkey families,' for a prize of a frozen Turkey.

"Then we had refreshments and the party was over. Now I could go back to real life. It was a bigger job than I had imagined beforehand. But very, very satisfying."

· 14 ·

Basic Information

WHAT IS A SCHOOL TURN-OFF?

A School Turn-Off is an official project involving all members of a school community—administrators, teachers, and, of course, students and their families, who are encouraged to eliminate television viewing for a period of a week.

In one way the School Turn-Off is simply an expanded version of a Classroom Turn-Off: though there are many classes involved, each participating teacher follows the same rules and rituals outlined for the Classroom Turn-Off in part III. A classroom teacher involved in a School Turn-Off, however, has an advantage over the teacher organizing the experiment for one class alone: all the necessary materials for the Turn-Off—the charts, Battle Plans, contracts, etc., will be provided by those organizing the experiment. (Teachers of children in the lower grades follow the plan for the Early Childhood Turn-Off in part IV.)

It is in its organization and planning that the School Turn-Off differs considerably from its smaller versions. There are faculty meetings, parents' meetings, committee meetings, and the Recognition Day party to schedule, plan, and organize as well as materials for the various classroom activities—diaries, contracts, charts, and graphs—to coordinate and distribute to many classes. All this requires more paperwork: memos, invitations, letters to parents, letters to teachers, letters to kids, press releases, reminders, permissions; all have to be written, duplicated, distributed, sent out, collected. For the organizer, the Classroom Turn-Off seems a breeze by comparison.

But there is another difference that helps compensate for the extra effort. While a Classroom or an Early Childhood Turn-Off is an enlightening but essentially private experience, the School Turn-Off has the potential for becoming a dramatic public event. Because television is such an important part of everyone's life, the mere fact that a large group of people are willing to give it up, albeit briefly, becomes a newsworthy event. Consequently, with a certain amount of promotion, your Turn-Off will attract attention outside your school community—probably more than you imagine, and possibly more than you can easily handle.

The interest of the outside world, however, is one of the great advantages of the School Turn-Off. It adds immeasurably to the excitement of the event, fostering in all participants a heady sense of being involved in something valuable and important. If the world at large is so amazed by the fact that they are *not* watching television, children come to feel that there must be something to the idea that *not* watching television carries with it some significant advantages.

This section of the book provides a plan for the organization of a School Turn-Off. It suggests ideas for promotion and publicity, and for the fund-raising you will probably need to cover the expenses of this more ambitious event. But please remember: the School Turn-Off is only an organizational entity, a framework within which many smaller Turn-Offs take place simultaneously. For the actual activities and rituals to follow in their classrooms, as well as for suggested ways to sell the Turn-Off idea to parents and children involved, participating teachers will need to follow the Classroom Turn-Off or the Early Childhood Turn-Off format as outlined in parts III or IV of this book, with the exception of two new rituals that have been devised for this larger experiment—the All-School Kick-off Ceremony at its start and the Recognition Day party at its conclusion.

WHO TAKES PART?

Although a full-fledged School Turn-Off is an official enterprise approved and supported by the school's administration, participation by teachers and students must be voluntary. Involvement will depend to a great degree on the interest and leadership of individual classroom teachers: some teachers will join in with great enthusiasm and inspire their entire classroom to participate in the Turn-Off; others will choose to pay little notice to the event and its related activities.

By its very existence, however, the Turn-Off is likely to have an effect on everyone in the school, whether they actually join or not, if only by stimulating thought about television and the ways it affects people's lives.

THE PERSON IN CHARGE

To run a large-scale Turn-Off you need someone who has a gut feeling that this is very, very important. I have two children, ages 5 and 6, so I was concerned not only as an educator, but as a parent.
—Martha Thornton, librarian, organizer of the
Marshall, Missouri, Turn-Off

The person in charge of the School Turn-Off, usually the one who was inspired to start the project in the first place, who coordinates its various activities and sees it through to the end—that special person is the crucial ingredient that determines its success.

If you were to come into a gathering of people who have organized successful Turn-Offs in their schools or communities, you might not easily detect a common denominator among them: they are young or old, male or female, dynamic or shy, parents, teachers, or librarians.

What they share, you would discover on closer acquaintance, is an unwavering belief in the importance of focusing attention on television's negative impact on learning and family life. They also share a strong sense of mission about the importance of books and reading. Finally, they all possess an indispensable set of personal qualities: energy, perseverance, tenacity, and a rare ability to function calmly in the midst of chaos.

If you are considering the idea of organizing a School Turn-Off, it is important to be forewarned: you're taking on a big job. But it is equally important to know that it does not call for any particular organizational genius, merely doggedness, hard work, and confidence in the importance of the idea.

· 15 ·

Get Ready:
Organizing a School Turn-Off

SELLING THE TURN-OFF TO THE STAFF

Persuading the Principal

Persuading the school principal of the value of a TV Turn-Off is a necessary first step in organizing a School Turn-Off, and it is not always the easiest one. If you are a teacher or librarian or school parent, even though you have come to believe that a TV Turn-Off is a great idea, your principal or headmaster may need convincing.

Make an appointment for a meeting and go equipped with ammunition to defend the Turn-Off idea. (The arguments in chapter 1 outlining the negative impact of TV viewing on school achievement and family life will be helpful.) Or simply use "What's Wrong with Watching TV?" (page 154) and "Why a TV Turn-Off" (page 155) as the basis for your sales pitch, perhaps leaving a copy of the pages on the principal's desk for later reading.

Once you've received official approval of the project, you'll need the principal's help in setting an official date for the Turn-Off. Try to pick a week that is four to six months in advance to give you adequate time for planning all the necessary meetings, for ordering or making the various Turn-Off accessories—the buttons, contracts, viewing charts, and diaries and distributing them to the classrooms, and for tracking down prizes for the Recognition Day party, as well as for the fund-raising you'll need to do to help raise money for all these things. Most of all, you'll need time for publicizing the event. It may seem a long way off when you first set the date, but you'll be glad of every extra day as the Turn-Off approaches.

Avoid the week immediately *before* or *after* a school vacation;

or the week of some particularly exciting and much-heralded national, community, or media event such as the World Series or a major election. The principal should check the school calendar and make sure the date you are considering does not coincide with any forthcoming school event that might interfere with the Turn-Off activities.

Before you finish your meeting with the principal, ask to have time at the next staff meeting to present the Turn-Off idea to the faculty.

Persuading the Teachers

After you have "sold" the Turn-Off to the principal, present the idea as persuasively as you can at the next full staff meeting. Again, you may use the collection of quotes from other Turn-Offs: "Why a TV Turn-Off" (page 155) and the arguments in "What's Wrong with Watching TV?" (page 154) to help you explain the underlying purpose of the experiment, perhaps distributing copies of these pages to all teachers attending for reading at their leisure. But it's important to be aware that selling the idea of a Turn-Off to the teachers in your school and enlisting their enthusiastic cooperation may be harder than you think.

While most teachers today *are* concerned about television and its effects on children's school achievement, many continue to focus their efforts on influencing children to watch better programs rather than trying to persuade them to reduce viewing hours. These and others who have come to take an "If-you-can't-beat-'em-join-'em" approach and who use television as an educational adjunct, will find the TV Turn-Off idea threatening. If you are to gain their cooperation in your planned School Turn-Off, you will need to raise their consciousness somewhat.

Describe the Classroom Turn-Off Plan, using the step-by-step outline on page 84, and explain that it has been tried successfully in other schools. Be sure you mention that all materials for the various Turn-Off rituals and activities—the forms for viewing charts, Battle Plans, contracts, the buttons, diaries, etc., will be provided for all participating teachers, as well as suggestions for how to sell the idea to the kids in their classes. Emphasize that a Turn-Off can be an enjoyable experience for the kids, an adventure akin to camping in the wilderness, rather than a terrible deprivation.

You will not persuade everyone, but you will certainly find a number of valuable allies at this meeting. These will generally be the teachers who become most involved in the Turn-Off and who participate most creatively and enthusiastically in their classrooms.

Follow-up Letter to Teachers about the Turn-Off

Since some teachers may have been absent from the staff meeting at which the Turn-Off idea was introduced, and others may have been present but for any number of reasons unreceptive to the idea that day, send a follow-up letter to the entire staff, outlining the details of the event, making it sound like fun, and emphasizing the importance of their participation. Make it clear that the Turn-Off will not involve a great deal of extra work for them: all the necessary materials will be provided. A model for such a letter may be found on page 186.

Make sure that this letter includes a tear-off coupon on which teachers may indicate whether they plan to participate with their class or not. Those teachers who do not return their coupon may need another follow-up, perhaps in person, at which time you may try another sales pitch to get them to join in.

SELLING THE TURN-OFF TO THE PARENTS

Involving the P.T.A.

It is important to make a great effort to reach as many parents in your school as possible, and encourage them to participate in the Turn-Off together with their children. Only if the school parent body understands the underlying purpose of the experiment and stands behind it can the lessons of the Turn-Off work to effect real change.

For this purpose, the Parent-Teacher Association is your logical ally. The concerned parents who are active in such an organization will be helpful in gaining the support of a network of parents who are involved in school affairs and who can help you with some of the difficult logistics of the project. The P.T.A. can also be most helpful in setting up the all-important Parents' Meeting about Television, at which you present the Turn-Off idea to your school's parent body.

How do you gain the P.T.A.'s support and approval? Start with the president, and sell the idea to him or her. Then ask to address the executive committee, and sell the idea to them. You'll be getting some good experience in the art of persuasion, experience that will come in handy when you have to convince a larger group to join the TV Turn-Off at the parents' meeting about television.

Planning a Parents' Meeting

An evening parents' meeting on the subject of television is the most effective way to gain interest and support for a TV Turn-Off among your parent body.

It always helps to have an additional drawing card—a child psychologist, for instance, or educator who might speak briefly on the need for television control. Another attraction for a parents' meeting might be a panel of veterans from other Turn-Offs who can describe their own experiences with a No-TV Week, attest to the benefits of such an experiment, and answer questions from the audience. You will find a model for a notice for a parents' meeting on page 178.

In case you have to carry the burden of explanation and persuasion yourself, you will find some helpful suggestions in the section "A Parents' Meeting about Television" on page 179.

A Follow-up Letter

Obviously not all parents will be able to go to the parents' meeting, and yet you want your entire parent body to be informed about the Turn-Off. On page 181 you will find a model for a follow-up letter (with a Spanish translation) to be distributed to children in all classrooms to take home to their parents. It is important to have this letter come from the school principal if possible, for added authority. It is also advisable to include a coupon at the bottom for children to return to their classroom teachers with a parent's signature.

· 16 ·

Get Set: Preparing for the Turn-Off

COMMITTEES

The more responsibility you can allocate to capable committees, the smoother and easier your Turn-Off will be. The meetings with teachers and parents at which you present the idea of a School Turn-Off are your best opportunities to sign up enthusiastic volunteers for Turn-Off committees.

Suggestions follow for committees that should be established at least a month before your Turn-Off. Keep in mind that a perfectly functional committee may be composed of one reliable and hard-working person.

• The Publicity Committee: Prepares and sends off press releases to local newspapers, radio stations, etc., before the Turn-Off and a summary of Turn-Off results at its conclusion; coordinates media requests for interviews—prepares a list of families available for newspaper, radio, or TV interviews. (Anybody in the school community with press, radio, or TV connections is, of course, a valuable asset to this committee.)

• The Entertainment Committee: Coordinates the Recognition Day party, prepares refreshments, organizes entertainment and speeches, prepares certificates of merit and prizes to be presented at party.

• The Education Committee (a committee of parents and teachers): Helps plan classroom activities for the Turn-Off; helps assemble and then distribute the various Turn-Off materials to classrooms.

DISTRIBUTING MATERIALS TO THE CLASSROOMS

Every classroom participating in the School Turn-Off will need certain basic materials—charts, contracts, etc.—to follow the Classroom Turn-Off Plan. Models of these documents have been provided in the Nuts and Bolts section of the appendix on page 167. The pages should be duplicated in large enough quantities for all participating classes in the Turn-Off and then distributed two weeks before the Turn-Off is scheduled to begin.

For each participating classroom you will need:
One for each child in the class:

1. Follow-up Letter to Parents (see page 181).
2. Letter to Kids taking Part in a TV Turn-Off (see page 171).
3. Viewing chart (two for each child—one for week before Turn-Off and one for follow-up a month later (see page 168).
4. Battle Plan forms (see page 169).
5. Contracts (see page 174).
6. Follow-up questionnaires (see page 184).
7. Turn-Off diaries (see page 173).
8. No-TV buttons (see page 173).

Each teacher will need a packet of instructions including:

1. Selling a TV Turn-Off to Kids (see page 159).
2. The Kick-off Ceremony (see page 176).
3. Classroom Activities and Assignments (see page 183).
4. Turn-Off accessories (see page 173).

You will also need a Turn-Off Survival Kit, for each family planning to join their children in the Turn-Off.

LETTING THE WORLD KNOW

You are involved in an exciting project. Why not create a bit of a stir about it in your community? Here's how to begin:

1. You will want to send a press release to all your local newspapers, radio stations, and TV stations, and to some magazines as well. Address the release to the city editor of the papers and to the news desk of the radio and TV stations.

2. If you live in a large city, send your release to the large press services too, such as U.P.I. and A.P. Find out by telephone how to get your event on their "day list" on the day the Turn-Off is scheduled to begin.

3. Time your mailing to have your release arrive about a week before the event for daily papers and news programs, and, if you are extremely well organized, about a month in advance for any weekly publications or general interest monthly magazines.

You'll find a sample press release on page 192. You may want to send an additional press release after your Turn-Off is over to summarize for the press how well it succeeded. Include here the number of participants, the attendance at Recognition Day, the names of participating community organizations, and the names of businesses who contributed to the Turn-Off.

FUND-RAISING

No matter how "no-frills" you envision your Turn-Off to be, you'll still be faced with a surprising number of unavoidable expenses—printing or mimeographing costs, carfare, stationery, stamps, posterboard, the No-TV buttons, refreshments for parents' meetings, and, the biggest expense of all, refreshments and prizes for Recognition Day—you'll be amazed at how all these add up in a School Turn-Off.

Unless your school is willing to allocate special funds for this worthy project, your School Turn-Off will probably require some fund-raising. Here are some suggestions:

1. There are, of course, the usual fund-raising strategies—bake sales, paperback book fairs, lotteries, etc.

2. You can apply for direct support to local service organizations such as the Elks or Lions or Kiwanis clubs, many of which have

special funds for worthy community projects. Most of these clubs and organizations have weekly meetings, usually at lunch time. Call and ask for the program chairman and request an appointment to address a club meeting in the near future. Go equipped with your most persuasive arguments (see "What's Wrong with Watching TV?" and "Why a TV Turn-Off" on pages 154 and 155.

If you live in a smaller community, many of the members of these organizations will also be parents of children in your school. Your "sales pitch" at a meeting may do more than get you a financial contribution: it may create allies for your Turn-Off who will become enthusiastic participants themselves.

3. You may also apply to local businesses for contributions and donations of suitable prizes for Recognition Day. The most likely prospects are those whose business may somehow be improved as a result of the Turn-Off. A bookstore is a good example of a business that stands to profit by a reduction in TV viewing time. Indeed, one Midwest community even chose to call its TV Turn-Off "Turn Off TV—Bring on the Books!" Other good candidates for supporting a Turn-Off are toy and hobby stores, record stores, children's clothing stores, fast-food chains (many of these have an active community-relations program and will be interested in a project such as a TV Turn-Off), and various enterprises involving free-time activities, such as skating rinks, bowling alleys, or golf driving ranges. A model letter soliciting help from merchants and businesses may be found on page 197.

GETTING OFFICIAL APPROVAL AND RECOGNITION

A helpful step to ensure larger participation in the Turn-Off is to obtain the official approval of the Board of Education and community officials in the form of official proclamations or resolutions. This may be a crucial factor in convincing some parents to participate, and it will certainly help in soliciting financial contributions from community businesses and service organizations.

You'll find examples of proclamations and resolutions used in other TV Turn-Offs on page 195.

ENLISTING COMMUNITY INVOLVEMENT

The more involvement and cooperation of community organizations you can muster for your TV Turn-Off, the more excitement you will generate and the greater the potential for widespread participation. Send an announcement letter soliciting participation and help to all the organizations you can think of—among the most obvious: the Girl Scouts, the Boy Scouts, 4-H Clubs, Future Farmers, historical societies, local cultural organizations, drama groups. Invite leaders of these groups to a planning meeting, and enlist them in organizing special activities during the TV Turn-Off week.

Involving a large number of community groups with your TV Turn-Off may serve many useful purposes. These groups may be able to provide exciting activities for the Turn-Off week, and they can spread the word about the TV Turn-Off. Most important, if a group becomes officially involved with the TV Turn-Off, its members and their families are far more likely to become willing participants themselves! Therefore, the final reason for soliciting the involvement of community groups is to increase the numbers of people actually "turning off."

A model of a letter to community groups may be found on page 196.

Go!
The School Turn-Off and After

THE ALL-SCHOOL KICK-OFF CEREMONY

Start the School Turn-Off with a bang at an All-School Kick-off Ceremony to be held on the first day of the event, perhaps in place of the weekly school assembly. Include recitations of poems about TV, skits, a talent show (billed as a demonstration of skills and talents that thrive in the absence of TV), and end with a dramatic, symbolic shrouding of a TV set. (See the "Kick-off Ceremony for the Classroom" on page 177.)

While this ceremony lends itself to a certain levity, the Kick-off Ceremony must combine lightness with gravity. A few words by the principal, or an enthusiastic teacher, librarian, or parent about the serious purpose of the experiment will start No-TV Week off with the feeling of importance it deserves.

CONTESTS

There are a number of contests your school may hold during the Turn-Off week. These serve a triple purpose. By offering a prize as well as the joy of winning, a contest gives kids an added incentive to join the Turn-Off. By encouraging children to be active—to write, draw, take photographs, and so forth—a contest helps children discover the fulfillment that comes from "doing" rather than "viewing," a major goal of the Turn-Off itself. Finally, a contest serves as an important publicity adjunct: your local newspapers, large or small, are likely to take an interest in contest entries, and may choose to print them—yet another thrilling incentive for contestants.

The most popular contest is a simple essay contest—"What I did during the Turn-Off," or "What I learned by Turning off the TV," or similar topics. Other possible contests are a photography contest, a drawing or painting contest, a poster contest (the winner to be used in publicizing the Turn-Off)—all with some No-TV theme. Try to have as many prizes as possible—for the funniest, the most dramatic, the most artistic, and so on.

Here are some excerpts from prizewinning essays from a number of TV Turn-Offs in different parts of the country.

Walden Revisited

While not Thoreau's two years, two months and two days at Walden Pond, the Turn-Off was one week of challenge. . . .

What I discovered in this venture in a more primitive, Thoreau-like life, life without TV, are priceless lessons:

1. The lives of most interest to me are the lives of my family and friends. Time for them must be first priority. Turn off TV.

2. Without the dulling drone of TV, one develops a sharper sensitivity to more delicate sights and sounds: the song of the birds at the feeder, the winds swirling the leaves, the snow on the November-blooming forsythia. Turn off TV.

3. Silence. I like it! It renews me. Turn off TV.

4. Reading, thought, meditation. There is time for these without TV and I recognize my need if I'm to grow. Turn off TV.

5. Creative efforts give me a sense of fulfillment. (What creative thought ever entered my mind watching TV?) What did I create this week? A new recipe, a cross-stitch design, this essay, a slide set narration, a project application. Would I have created these in a "normal" week? One, perhaps. Turn off TV. . . .

And finally, "TV Turn-Off week" gave me the opportunity to revisit Walden and rediscover its appeal. Would I have reread it otherwise. No! You see—"Turn off TV!"

—Karen Montgomery, Richmond, Indiana, Turn-Off:
Prizewinner—adult category

Confessions of a Turnip

This is a true confession of a TV addict. I could watch TV all day and then all night. I could always find something to watch. My mother thought she was raising three children and a turnip (that's me). Then came "cold turkey" and the TV was silent and blank. The first few days I was in a state of shock—my body moved but something was unusual in my mind. My "mini-screen eyes" were focusing on games, puzzles, books, etc. My ears were listening to new sounds, like the sound of my sled runners crunching through the snow. My senses were returning. . . .

—From prizewinning essay by Brian Kelly, sixth grade, Farmington, Connecticut, Turn-Off

We'll Watch TV Again . . . But . . .

How did we do? Well, it wasn't a problem to turn to books as a pastime. We pulled out games which were gathering dust. We did some housecleaning (not too much, mind you). We were noisy. The children were more pleasant, more cooperative with us and with one another. My husband did not pledge, but he cut down. When he did watch, it was after the children's bedtime and when I was not around.

Who knew what the following week would bring? Would abstinence make the heart grow fonder? In fact, I found more selection in TV viewing. There was not the usual mad rush to the family room to see what we were or were not missing. We spent time outdoors raking leaves, getting ready for winter. My husband took the children bowling—a previously once-a-year activity. Music lessons were practiced a little less grudgingly.

We'll watch TV again—we enjoy it. But we'll remember a week of primitive life when we were challenged to do without—cold turkey.

—The conclusion of a winning essay by a parent in Richmond, Indiana

RECOGNITION DAY

The culmination of a School Turn-Off comes at Recognition Day, when the successful completion of the experiment is celebrated and recognized in some way. Each child who signed a contract receives a prize at this occasion, and each family a certificate of merit commemorating their survival in this difficult and challenging experiment. (See page 190 for a model certificate of merit.)

In addition to prizes and certificates, Recognition Day offers participants an opportunity to share their Turn-Off experiences with one another and with the world at large. Invite parents to say a few words, encourage teachers who were most actively involved to speak, and choose a number of children to read excerpts from their Turn-Off diaries. (Be sure you include an honest cross section of children's comments—those describing a terrible struggle not to watch TV as well as those who describe their discoveries of new activities.) You might want to have two or three kids alternate reading a collection of "Desperation Time-Fillers" from No-TV diaries, such as the one that follows this section.

Of course a party is not a party without music and refreshments. You can have anything from a live band to a small phonograph with dance records; and from a giant cake in the shape of a television set to a few platters of cookies.

The entertainment at Recognition Day should, of course, stick to the theme of television. Kids may put on skits of their choosing, read or recite poems or sing songs. Winners of contests should read their essays and hold up their photos or posters. But don't feel limited by the television theme. Any sort of demonstration of talent—dancing, playing a musical instrument, acrobatics—may be included on the program as a demonstration of the kinds of skills that people can develop when they turn off the TV. Anything goes, as long as it's live, active, and doesn't appear on a screen.

Some communities include a lottery as part of Recognition Day, to help cover expenses. The ideal prize? A cold (frozen) turkey, naturally!

(An organizational plan for a Recognition Night party is given on page 188.)

TWENTY-FOUR DESPERATION
TIME-FILLERS FROM NO-TV DIARIES

1. Dear Diary: Friday—It was a pretty boring day until I had a fight with my sister who played the piano and she kept on kicking me.

2. Friday—After school, since I didn't have anything to do because of No-TV I did my homework. After that I took a long bath. Then I brushed my hair. Then I swept my grandmother's house.

3. Activities from diary: Cut out magazine pictures, read bedtime stories, went with my mother to the supermarket, did pudding for me and my sister, called my friend and played board games, washed clothes with my mother, played with my minipad, pencil, and lipstick eraser, did crochet, did exercises, played games, drew pictures, went for a walk, and bought some things, did an experiment in my workbook of science, played with my sister's play boat, organized my room, did my homework, went to the store to look around.

4. 4/23: Today when I got home I finished 2 drawings that I did. After that I started organizing my room. The thing I did was fix my bed, sweep, and fixed the teddy bear. Then I heard the radio. When I started to hear the radio I was thinking about going to the movies and seeing "9 Deaths of the Ninja." When I finished that I did a lot of exercises. After that I cleaned the bathroom. It almost took me an hour. Then I started to read a book. It is called "The Sendai." I read half of the chapter of my book.

5. 4/28: What I did instead of TV: sweep my house; did a 3D flower; play board games with my friend; made play-dough for my 3D flower; in evening, had a party; played games with my friends; went to sleep.

6. Day 3 of No-TV Week: First I did crochet. I used color, white and black. I did a big bracelet and a chain. Then my friend Eileen wanted to play dice. If the number from the dice is one, then the other player has to get number 2. Then the other player has to get 3. The game keeps on and on. In the evening I called my friend. We talked about what we were going to do for our vacation. Then I called my other friend Farrah. We were talking about No-TV

Week. My friend said that she don't like it. After I called my friends I played jump-rope. I jumped 100 times. Then I watched TV. And at 9 o'clock I went to bed.

7. No-TV Journal—Friday: I did knitting 5 times. The first time it came out not that good. But then I got used to it. I played jump rope outside the balcony. Then I tooked a bath. After I tooked a bath I ate supper. The food was white rice, chicken and potatoes. When I finish eating, I sat down on the sofa and talk to my friends. Then I did more of knitting. When I finish knitting, I read some books. Some books were scary, and some books were fun. I enjoyed most "Joji Bear Ghost of a Chance." It talked about a haunted set of furniture. After that I was hearing the TV. That wasn't fun at all, so I did exercise.

8. Instead of watching TV I helped make dinner, and I usually don't.

9. I came home from school and I didn't watch TV. I just took a little rest and I was talking to my mommy.

10. 8:p.m.—Looked for batteries. Stared into space. Didn't miss television.

11. I went to bed a half hour earlier.

12. Dear Diary: I was at my uncle's house and everybody was watching TV. I stayed in the kitchen and read and made a cake.

13. I have taken funny pictures from the New Yorker Magazine for a scrapbook.

14. Instead of watching TV I had a long talk about school.

15. Dear Diary: I got up at 6 a.m. Then I just sat there.

16. 11:43 to 12:15—I fought with my brother Kevin. 6:30 to 6:45—I counted my money.

17. Dear Diary: first I moped the bathroom. Then I talked on my CB for a while.

18. After supper I thought about things for a long time.

19. Today instead of watching TV, I washed out my thermos.

20. Today instead of watching TV I wrote on my brother's feet and stomach.

21. Today I fought with my brother for 30 minutes.

22. Today I stared into space for a while.

23. Today I went to the YMCA, came home, ate dinner, got fed up and went to bed.

24. Dear Diary: tried to kiss Arielle but I could not. But I will try Monday.

▪ EVERYTHING YOU NEED ▪
FOR A SCHOOL TURN-OFF

You'll find most of the materials you'll need for organizing and running a School Turn-Off—model letters, plans for meetings, etc, in the appendix at the end of this book, as well as all the various forms for the individual Classroom Turn-Offs that make up the School Turn-Off. The Step-by-step Checklist for a School Turn-Off, which follows, will refer you to the pages where you will find the necessary material for every stage of the event.

Step-by-step Checklist for a School Turn-Off

1. Sell Turn-Off idea to school principal.
2. Choose suitable date for Turn-Off.
3. Sell Turn-Off idea to school staff at staff meeting.
4. Send Follow-up letter to teachers (page 186).
5. Get cooperation of P.T.A.
6. Plan an evening parents' meeting about television (pages 178 and 179).
7. Organize committees.
8. Distribute all necessary material for Classroom Turn-Off to each participating class. (Each teacher will then follow step-by-step outline for Classroom Turn-Off on page 84.)
10. Send out press releases to newspapers, radio, TV (pages 192 and 193).
11. Proceed with fund-raising at local service organizations and businesses (page 197).
12. Get official approval of Turn-Off from Board of Education (page 195).
13. Enlist community involvement (page 196).
14. During Week of the Turn-Off:
    a. All-school Kick-off Ceremony on first day (page 177).
    b. Contests (page 122).
    c. Recognition Day—at end of Turn-Off (pages 187 and 188).

·Part VI·

TV Turn-Off
Variations

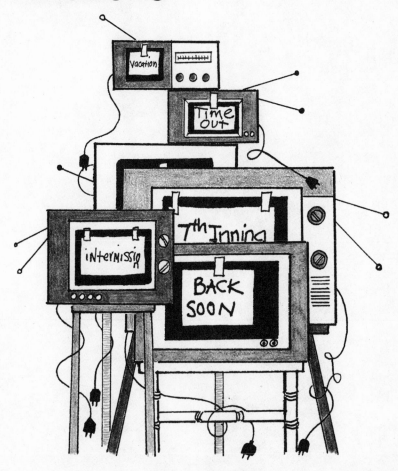

·18·

All Sorts of Turn-Offs

This chapter summarizes a number of alternative No-TV experiments without giving a detailed plan for their reenactment at home or in school. Some may be too ambitious for most readers to even contemplate and others too specialized or too limited to seem appealing. Nevertheless, they have been used effectively by some families, schools, and communities throughout the country and are worth consideration. Or they may inspire you to create an entirely new Turn-Off variation to suit your own particular purposes.

A COMMUNITY TV TURN-OFF

A Community TV Turn-Off differs from smaller No-TV experiments mainly in size and organizational complexity: this is not merely a large and ambitious project, it is an enormous project that coordinates various segments of an entire community—families, classrooms, schools, libraries—all simultaneously involved in a Turn-Off. It requires the expenditure of enormous amounts of time and energy from its organizers, but thanks to the inevitable publicity that attends such events, its potential for alerting a large number of people to the need for television control is similarly enormous.

In recent years, a number of successful community Turn-Offs have enjoyed an unusual amount of public attention. In Piscataway, New Jersey, the month of April, 1985, was officially inaugurated as "Turn Off the TV Month" when the mayor of the town switched off the television set at the John F. Kennedy Memorial Library on April 1. Jane Kucharski, community service librarian at the Piscataway public library, together with Robin del Giudice, children's librarian, initiated the idea, basing it on the Farmington model. An eight-person committee made up of school officials, P.T.A. officials, librarians, and members of the local business and cultural arts communities worked on its planning and organization.

Eight hundred pledge cards were signed, and 561 families handed in their cards at the end of the month, indicating that they had succeeded in turning off their TVs for one week or more during the month of April. The total for a month-long "cold turkey" from television was 132.

In Richmond, Indiana, Sue Weller (a librarian at the Morrison Reeves Library), organized the "Turn Off TV—Bring on the Books" Week, to coincide with National Book Week, November 12–18, 1984. A total of 1,158 area residents reported that they did not watch television at all for the entire seven days, while 143 others reported they had cut down on their viewing during the Turn-Off.

But by far the most ambitious and the most famous community Turn-Off took place in Farmington, Connecticut.

THE FARMINGTON TURN-OFF

The Farmington Turn-Off was held during the month of January, 1984. Of the 17,000 residents of this handsome suburb of Hartford, more than 4,000 reported drastic reduction in their TV viewing during the month-long Turn-Off; 1,047 Farmingtonians actually went "cold turkey" and eliminated TV entirely during the Turn-Off.

The mammoth organization job was carried off by Nancy DeSalvo, a children's librarian and the president of the Farmington Library Council as well as a mother of six children, a remarkable woman who almost single-handedly gathered support for the Turn-Off in the library and public school system and ran the month-long event from its first planning stages to its triumphant conclusion.

The Farmington Turn-Off attracted considerable attention:

newspapers and magazines from all over the United States as well as from England, France, and Israel sent reporters to cover the event. TV crews from every major network went to Farmington to interview parents and children, as did scores of radio interviewers fascinated by the extraordinary idea of voluntary abstinence from TV viewing. The final proof of success of the Farmington Turn-Off was the fact that it was repeated the following year, in January, 1985, and was equally successful.

THE LIBRARY—AN IDEAL TURN-OFF PARTNER

Although many different groups take part in a Community Turn-Off, there must be a single organizational center for the event. A library is ideally suited for such a central position not only because of its natural interest in enlarging children's horizons and promoting family well-being but also because one of the chief aims of a Turn-Off—to encourage reading and give it a chance to flourish in the absence of TV—is inextricably connected with the library's well-being, if not its very survival.

It is not surprising, therefore, that virtually all of the large-scale Community Turn-Offs that have been organized in various locations in recent years have, indeed, taken place under the aegis of a library system, often timed to coincide with National Children's Book Week. While most of these Turn-Offs have enjoyed the close cooperation of the community's school system, their success has depended to a great degree on the resources and authority of the library and on the remarkable leadership of such inspired librarians as Nancy DeSalvo, Jane Kucharski, Robin del Giudice, or Sue Weller.

In recent years a number of successful Community Turn-Offs—notably ones in Farmington, Connecticut, and Piscataway, New Jersey, have enjoyed an unusual amount of public attention. Smaller library-centered Turn-Offs in Marshall, Missouri, and Richmond, Indiana, were equally successful, if less widely publicized. A list of a number of special activities that may be organized by a public library during a TV Turn-Off is included on page 189 of the appendix.

A ONE-DAY SCHOOL TURN-OFF

Perhaps because the idea of missing just a single day of TV viewing is relatively non-terrifying, an amazing number of children—10,000—signed pledges to observe a TV Blackout on December 16, 1985, in Riverdale, New York, School District 10.

The organizers described two goals they hoped to achieve by means of the TV Blackout: "to focus attention on the power television holds over our lives" and "to gain insight into how to get control of the tube."

They succeeded splendidly with their first goal, and surprisingly well with the second, given the very brief duration of the No-TV period.

On December 16, newspaper reporters and television cameras descended in droves on District 10's schools and homes just as they had flocked to cover the much longer and more elaborate events in Farmington and Piscataway. A TV crew from NBC News arrived at one of the local schools and stayed for an hour, interviewing teachers and children about their amazing "ordeal." Certainly the purpose of focusing attention on television and its attendant problems was most successfully achieved, although, ironically, through the instrument of television itself.

Although the event came and went in a day, its impact on a number of families began before December 16, and lasted long after. One mother, for instance, unaware of the extent of her son's dependence on television, was shocked to hear his response to the idea of a Blackout: "What! No TV? I can't live that way! Impossible!" The family began to take immediate steps to combat TV addiction: three weeks before the Blackout they began to do without TV one day each week, and continued to follow that pattern indefinitely. The parents discovered that having regular days without TV gave them some time "just to talk" with their two sons, while the children found themselves listening to music, playing board games, or just "acting like kids like to act" on their TV-less evenings, as their father cheerfully described it.

During the brief Blackout a number of parents made less startling but nevertheless useful discoveries that would affect their subsequent attitudes and use of TV. Some commented on the unprecedented peace and quiet that settled over their home in the absence of television's sound. Others noted a feeling of having more time to do things. One father, for example, repaired a picture frame, a small job he had been putting off for months: suddenly he had time on his hands.

At yet another home in which television had been unplugged for the Blackout, parents and children agreed that dinnertime was much more satisfying without the TV on and decided to keep the TV off during meals from then on.[7]

TV BUSTERS: A FUND-RAISING TURN-OFF

"Can 1,000 or more elementary school children turn off their television sets for one week, cold turkey, even for a good cause?" asked the write-up in the *Hartford Courant*.

The idea, conceived by Arthur Levine, a director of the Muscular Dystrophy Association, was to organize an event similar to a walk-a-thon or a bike-a-thon, in which children collect pledges to receive a certain amount of money for every mile they walk or bicycle. This event, held during May 1985, in the the town of Billerica, Massachusetts, had a new twist, however: calling themselves TV Busters, the children collected pledges for each day they would manage to keep their TVs off completely.

And just as the walk-a-thons and bike-a-thons promote physical fitness while raising money for a worthy cause, this event too had a dual intention: though a prize was offered for the child who raised the most money, the organizers hoped that the best prize of all would be received by all the children involved—a chance to develop other interests besides the electronic screen.

The event was a huge success: over $17,500 was raised for MDA, while reading and family activities flourished in participating housholds, according to a survey taken at the time.

How did they ensure that the children really did "turn off" for the period they had pledged? Each child's parents were required to sign a verification slip that was shown to the donors before they made their contributions.[8]

No-TV on the Sabbath

The Rosemans, a young couple who have been married for two years, enjoy a once-a-week TV Turn-Off that is an important part of their Sabbath observance.

During the week television had been a minor but steady source of dissonance for Hannah and Joel Roseman.

"Joel used to watch a lot of TV," his wife reports. "He's selective, but if there's nothing on he likes he'll sometimes watch anyway. TV seems to be a sort of battery or lifeline for him. He says it helps him relax.

"I'll watch with him if there's something on that interests me. Otherwise I'll read. Sometimes, when the set is just on I say, 'Why don't you turn it off?' and he'll say 'I'm watching it,' or 'I'll watch it in a minute.' I think it's silly to have it on if you're not going to watch. Superfluous."

The Rosemans are Orthodox Jews, whose observance of the Sabbath follows strict rules, among them a rule forbidding the turning on or off of any appliance during the duration of the Sabbath, from sundown on Friday to sundown on Saturday.

In fact, there is no rule forbidding the actual *watching* of TV on the Sabbath and some observant families continue to avail themselves of TV on the Sabbath by using a timing device that automatically turns the set on and off at certain times.

"We had the clock," Hannah Roseman says, "and for the first few months of our marriage we did watch TV on the Sabbath. But our Sabbath observance is very important for us, and we began to feel that watching TV wasn't in consonance with the day and what we were trying to do—to let the world slip away and let us focus on more spiritual things. Instead, the television just brought in the world and all its conflicts. And so we decided not to watch on the Sabbath.

"At first it was really hard. After all, Friday night is prime time!" She laughs. "But slowly and painfully we broke the habit on that day. Now we talk more together, we read more, we work a bit at filling the time in a good way. And we're both very happy that we do it. I think it makes a difference for our marriage, and I know it makes a difference in the way Joel watches TV during the rest of the week. He doesn't seem quite so connected with the set."

A Family Turn-Off on a Bet

Mary Dixon, the founder of the Society for the Eradication of Television (SET), a growing anti-TV organization in Albuquerque, New Mexico, challenged her friend Joe Feather, who is a local policeman, to give up TV for a month. His story, which he wrote up for the SET newsletter, follows:

When Mary made a "gentleman's bet" with us to give up television for one month, I thought to myself, "This will be easy. I don't watch TV that much anyway." My wife was not so sure, but I resolutely turned the TV to the wall and waited to see what would happen.

The first thing I noticed was that I suddenly had a lot more time. Since I didn't regulate my life around the time when specific shows were on, I was able to do things without having to rush back to the house for a TV show. My wife and I played a lot more racketball and went out to eat more often. I also got to spend more time with my daughter, and was able to spend more time reading.

The break was not completely painless, unfortunately. I went into "news withdrawal" and began to buy two newspapers a day to make up for the loss of the evening news on television. I also felt an empty feeling on Thursday evenings when "Cheers" and "The Cosby Show" were on. I made up for this by joining a Thursday Racketball League. All of these withdrawal symptoms gradually diminished, however, until at the end of the month they were gone completely.

With my wife the break was even more complete. The "Wheel of Fortune" addict who was so unsure about going a month without television suddenly became virulently anti-television and talked about never turning it on again. I think both of us started to realize just how much TV we had been watching.

One of the things that we had noticed earlier was that our daughter, age one year, had been drawn to the TV screen like a magnet. Television made her placid and easy to deal with—but at what cost? During the month she became very attracted to books and magazines, played a lot more, and was easier to get to sleep.

We noticed this with a friend's daughter when we were house/baby-sitting for him and his wife. We were told that their 2-year-old was almost impossible to put to bed at night. Without TV, however, she played with our daughter all day and was completely worn out by bedtime. We had no problem putting her to bed at eight. She did not complain about not having TV either as long as we were doing something else with her.

The month without TV was an enlightening experience to say the least. Is our TV still turned to the wall? No, but it took us over a week after the month was over to turn it on again. I still watch the news and my wife still watches "Wheel of Fortune" but the TV does not come first any longer. We both exercise a lot more than we did and are more likely to do things away from home. I don't think that television is absolute evil incarnate but I do know that I have control over it; more important, I am willing to exercise that control.

If you really think that you have control over your television, try what I did. Take a month off. Go a month without TV and see how much control you really have over your television set.[9]

Conclusion

THE INERTIA FACTOR

The heavy force of inertia that causes us to resist change and keep doing things the way we've always done them generally serves to protect family well-being: by keeping things the same, it helps preserve stability, the crucial component upon which our comfort and sense of security depends. Only when a family settles into unhealthy or distinctly injurious patterns does this inertial force become a handicap. Then we find ourselves in a rut, as we say, and we need a push of some sort to help us achieve a needed change.

Often, other factors combine with the force of inertia to make change even harder to accomplish. A car deeply stuck in the mud, for example, requires more than a simple push to prevent it from sinking in even deeper. Similarly, a family trying to change a habit as addictive and passively gratifying as television viewing needs more than a TV Turn-Off to bring about permanent change. A break from television may provide the necessary initial push, but new and more favorable patterns must then be established if a family is not to settle right back into the same old comfortable grooves. As one parent ruefully put it, "The Turn-Off was great—we did so many things together, we really felt much more like a real family. But somehow or other we've slowly but surely drifted back to watching the same way we always did—too much."

FIRM RULES

How can families best take advantage of the "push" of a TV Turn-Off to overcome their natural inertia and bring about a needed change in their daily routine?

The answer lies in setting up and then maintaining new family rules about television. This, of course, is more easily said than done, as parents who have struggled steadily and unsuccessfully to control television know too well. Nevertheless, there's reason to believe that rules about TV use are easier to establish after a Turn-Off than before. While children may have greeted past efforts to enforce family rules with stolid resistance accompanied by genuine bewilderment about why this amusing pastime had to be curtailed, after a Turn-Off they have new insight into the addictive nature of TV viewing and a better grasp of its negative impact on family life. Hence they are less likely to be resentful and rebellious about firm rules governing TV use in the home.

But what rules to set? Here are a few possibilities:

Spot Improvement

A useful way to work on a family's television control problems might be called the "spot improvement method." It involves assessing the areas of most conspicuous improvement that come to light during the TV Turn-Off and then devising new rules that will serve to retain these changes.

You may have noticed, for example, that getting the children off to school was considerably easier during the No-TV period, and that breakfast was suddenly transformed into a pleasant family meal. A simple rule eliminating all morning TV watching will make these improvements permanent. If you are resolute about keeping this rule, you will probably meet with very little resistance, and perhaps even a bit of relief on the kids' part—*they* didn't enjoy the morning madhouse, either.

Similarly, if you found new enjoyment in family dinners during the Turn-Off, then following up with a non-negotiable rule about no-TV during meals makes sense for your family.

Did you discover that bedtime was much more peaceful when television and the "Just one more program!" plea were eliminated during a Turn-Off? Make a firm rule of "no-TV after 7:00" or whatever time your children begin to get ready for bed, with plenty of time thrown in for a good bedtime story. Then stick to this rule tenaciously. Make no exceptions, not even for "the most fantastic children's TV special ever." (It helps to bear in mind that "the most fantastic . . ." appears on the air with amazing regularity—every week or so!)

No Solitary TV Watching
Make TV viewing a special event that the whole family does together. No one may watch TV by him or herself.

Fewer "Regular" Programs
Limit everybody's watching to one or at the most two "regular" programs a week. This doesn't mean that family members may not watch more than one or two programs a week—but they may only watch one or two weekly series episodes. Not only does such a rule simply reduce the quantity of TV viewing, it also helps to discourage families from planning their weekly lives around the TV schedule.

No TV on School Days
For a family with school-age children, the easiest rule is simply: *No TV on school days.* That's it. No counting hours, no checking listings for the one or two permissible programs. No bargaining and haggling—"If I watch two hours today, I won't watch anything tomorrow," etc.

In this way television is effectively eliminated as a competitor for other, more fulfilling activities (lively family meals, conversations, games, reading aloud, and, of course, studying and doing homework) during a good chunk of the week. Then on weekends there is no restriction on TV viewing.

But won't the kids simply spend their entire weekends glued to the tube? Since so much of television viewing is done by habit, it is more likely that after five days without television they will forget about viewing for much of the weekend as well. The following case history gives a good picture of how a family comes to make a no-TV-on-school-days rule, and how it affects their lives:

"I Never Have to Nag about Homework Now"

Emily Bryant, a mother of three school-aged children, did not spend months agonizing about whether to establish a no-TV on-school-days rule in the Bryant household; she didn't even consult her husband Hank about it ("I knew he'd approve—he'd be happy if we got rid of the set entirely!"); she made the decision suddenly and impetuously one Wednesday afternoon in April when she went into her children's room and found them watching the "hundredth rerun" of a situation comedy. The room was a shambles. Penny, a sixth grader, had a report on Eskimos due the next day; Will, age nine, was lying on the floor, still wearing his school clothes, which were now enhanced with peanut butter and jelly from his snack; and Charles, age eight, a glazed look in his eye, did not even look up when she greeted him.

"That did it," she recalls. "I had a fit. I walked over to the set, clicked it off and said, 'This is going to stop right now. No more TV on school days!' "

"I knew I was being high-handed and unfair about it. Actually, I didn't really think I was going to stick to it. What amazed me was how little they protested. It was almost as if they'd been waiting for someone to draw the line. And so we kept it as a rule, and it's made a great difference to all of us, in many, many ways."

What are some of the changes in the Bryant household that they attribute to the no-TV-on-school-days rule?

"There's much more talking and doing—not necessarily with us parents, but with each other. Everybody seems calmer and cheer-fuller. And what's wonderful—I hardly ever have to nag and yell about homework now. It simply gets done—and not at the last minute either. Without TV on school days, in fact, the kids seem to spend much more time on homework, maybe because there isn't all that much else to do. But that's fine with me. I'm not afraid of a little boredom in their lives.

"Also," Mrs. Bryant adds after a small hesitation, "I watch a lot less TV myself now. Before the rule, the kids might have been watching TV in their room or the living room, and I would have been in the bedroom watching my programs. Now I'm more likely to do other things, or sit down and do things with them. And I have an exceptionally good feeling about that!"

Any problems with the no-TV-on-school-days rule?

"What bothers me," says Mrs. Bryant thoughtfully, "is that there's no middle ground. If you have a problem with too much candy eating you can say 'Well, you may have one candy bar a day,' but with TV there seems to be no other way besides simply eliminating it for chunks of time!"

What about weekends? When the limits are removed, do the children make up for their deprivation on school days by "pigging out" on TV? It doesn't seem to work out that way, according to Emily Bryant. "It's almost as if the habit were broken during the week," she says, "and they've gotten so used to doing other things that they forget about TV. Oh, they do watch on weekends! But I don't believe as much as before, even though they could theoretically watch all day."

Out the Window? Second Thoughts on TV

If you are still hesitant about abandoning a comfortable laissez-faire policy about family television and beginning a new sort of family life, one in which television plays a smaller role, you might be swayed by the following essay that appeared recently in the Denver Post. *The author, Dottie Lamm, is a parent and a psychiatric social worker, whose husband, Richard Lamm, is a former governor of Colorado. Although she spent many years in public life, her rueful observations about the role television played in her family life when her children were young, and the new rules she would set if she "had it all to do over," apply heartbreakingly to parents and families of every kind, and everywhere.*

Last week I heard a speech given by an author who is raising her two boys in a very old-fashioned manner—sans television! Through the years this woman has mothered and written (the former while the children were at home, the latter while they were at school) without the aid of a TV.

The reason I say "aid" is that I used the TV as exactly that—especially when my kids were little. I wasn't doing anything as grandiose as writing a novel, but I used it anyway. Turn on "Sesame Street"—call my volunteer phone list. Turn on "Electric Company"—read the newspaper.

And maybe I would still do that today, if I had preschoolers. With preschoolers, a parent has minimum time off but maximum control. Yet, I often find myself wishing we had thrown the TVs out the window once the kids entered school.

"You take the risk that your kids will feel culturally deprived," said the author Josephine Humphries, who took five years of "school hours" to write her recently published novel *Dreams of Sleep*.

For that reason, her children are allowed to watch TV at their grandparents' home on weekends; thus they can reiterate "Dukes of Hazzard" on Monday mornings and prove that they aren't complete social zombies.

"It's amazing what hobbies they have engaged in, and what talents they have developed, because we did *not* have TV at home," exclaimed Humphries.

Some child-development specialists have diagnosed the TV habit in certain kids as an actual addiction. With these kids, the *only* way to break the habit is to throw the TV out the window. Like an alcoholic, a TV addict has to stop "cold turkey." A "little" TV or "regulated" TV doesn't cut it.

Even when one's kids are not "addicts," regulating television can be a continual family crisis. We have gone through: (a) carefully picking the programs, (b) banning all daytime watching, (c) limiting the hours to 1½ hours per day.

But these methods were always breaking down when there were "educational specials." (Our kids got adept at tagging any newly advertised cartoon series as an "educational special.") Or when Christmas was approaching.

Or when the TVs in our house slowly multiplied from one to four. Or when we parents got distracted.

But the big problem in our house is not parental distraction, it's parental example! As politicians and current events "junkies," my husband and I have always had the TV on during breakfasttime. We are always "tuned in" right up to dinnertime (6:30 P.M.) and sometimes after dinner for the rest of MacNeil-Lehrer.

Television has had *some* educational and familial benefits. The whole family cleared its calendar to watch "Roots" and "Holocaust," and some of us were caught up in parts of "Centennial." Dick and Scott recently watched "Peter the Great." In the mid-seventies, Heather and I engaged in a Monday night mother/daughter "Little House on the Prairie" ritual for at least three consecutive years. And we all watch "60 Minutes."

But overall, television has been a familial and educational zero. When I think of all the hobbies, talents, Trivial Pursuit games, Boggle games, discussions, storytelling, and even substantive arguments that have literally gone down the "tube," I wince. Even now, with the added "advantage" of VCR and home movies.

In truth, if I had it all to do over, I guess I wouldn't have thrown the TV out the window. But here's what I would have done:

- Gotten rid of ancillary TV sets that can be carried around from kitchen to bedroom to basement.
- Kept only the one good large-screen color TV in the TV room.
- Bought a TV with a controllable access code, or a lock box with a key—early. (By the time the kids are driving cars and applying makeup, it's too late.)
- Opened the "box" or the "tube" only for important specials and specific news hours.
- Turned to National Public Radio for morning news and to "talking books" as background for boring, repetitive jobs.

Experts estimate that the television set in the typical American home is on for seven hours a day. Upon graduating from high school, the average student has spent more hours watching television than he or she has spent sitting in class—18,000 TV hours in all!

Although a recent evaluation of "Sesame Street" revealed that this particular program actually promotes reading readiness, excessive TV watching was found not only to take time away from reading but to contribute to the actual deterioration of reading skills.

So, at the risk of sounding "un-American," I've very belatedly concluded:

- Less TV is better than more.
- And "out the window" might not hurt.[10]

EXTREME MEASURES

Often those families who have the hardest time during their TV Turn-Off have the easiest time taking action afterward. The need for better television control becomes overwhelmingly clear to them as they suffer withdrawal pangs during the "cold turkey" period, and they begin to see that nothing short of extreme measures will allow them to accomplish this control.

Just as alcoholics come to understand that they are unable to drink in moderation, these families realize that they are unable to live successfully with television. After their TV Turn-Off, they begin to consider eliminating television from their homes altogether. Of course, this does not mean that they get rid of their TV sets immediately. Indeed, since a Turn-Off was clearly labeled as a *temporary* experiment, it would be unfair to suddenly announce that the Turn-Off was not just for a week, but forever! But once the decision is made, parents can begin to pave the way for the elimination of television at some chosen point in the future.

The most strategic time to eliminate TV is at the end of a fairly long "natural" No-TV period, such as a family vacation without TV, or a month or two at summer camp. The addictive pattern is already broken; the transition from a family life dominated by television to life without TV can be made under such circumstances with the least amount of misery.

Fighting the Passive Pull

Controlling television or even eliminating it from the home entirely will not, of course, automatically lead to family happiness. While television's addictive presence puts serious obstacles in the way of a fulfilling family life, its mere absence does not guarantee that parents and children will suddenly spend more time talking together or doing things together. For most of us there is always the passive pull to contend with, that deep-rooted inner force that too often makes it such an effort to pull ourselves together and be active—to plan a great dinner, to initiate a family game, to read aloud a story, to *do* something.

Television's attraction is so powerful precisely because it gratifies that passive side of human nature that all of us, adults and children, are endowed with in differing degrees. Consequently, an important step toward a more active and satisfying family life is to become aware of this passive pull, to assess its power, and to consciously struggle against it. For most parents this requires a deep commitment to family life, and a firm resolve to make their children's childhood a rich and distinctive experience that will serve as a resource for the rest of their lives, and as a model for their future experience as parents themselves. With television under control, this can become an achievable goal with an additional benefit: parenthood too becomes a more delightful, more fulfilling experience. A true commitment to the family, with the genuine struggle against passivity that this entails is far from easy. But the rewards are among the greatest life has to offer.

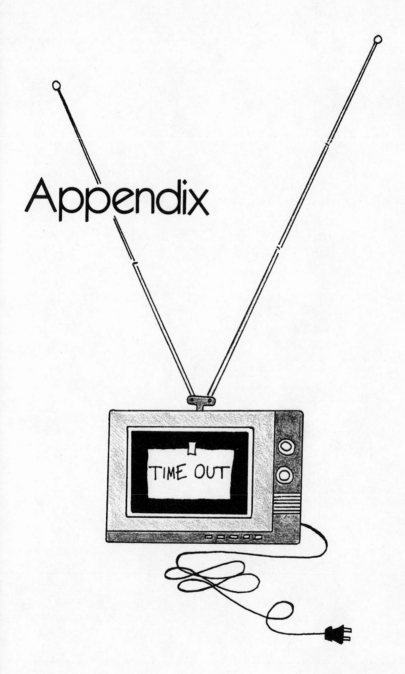

Appendix

TIME OUT

Appendix Contents

152 ·

A. The Turn-Off Survival Kit

For families engaging in a TV Turn-Off on their own, the following pages provide specific help in selling the Turn-Off idea to other family members, and hints for surviving the actual Turn-Off. Forms and models to copy and use for various Turn-Off rituals and activities are provided in the next section, "Nuts and Bolts."

Organizers of Turn-Offs may add to the Survival Kit any or all of the following:

1. Reading lists—good read-aloud books, preferably available at your school library.

2. Handouts from local museums, zoos, etc., with suggested cultural activities—things to do and places to go during Turn-Off week.

3. A list of names and phone numbers of families participating in the Turn-Off, for mutual support when the Turn-Off becomes difficult.

What's Wrong with Watching TV?
[Arguments to support the need for a TV Turn-Off]

1. TV takes time away from other more wholesome activities.
   (The actual time kids spend watching television is time *not* spent reading, playing, talking, etc.)

2. TV competes (and often wins) against alternative family activities.
   (Children will often reject activities such as listening to a story or playing a game in favor of the passive pleasures of TV.)

3. TV allows kids to grow up less civilized.
   (Parents do not work at socializing because they use TV to solve problems and keep children out of trouble.)

4. Television takes the place of play.
   (Just at the point when children are ready to acquire play skills, parents begin to use television as a baby-sitter.)

5. TV makes children less resourceful.
   (Kids who have grown up watching a lot of television have not had the opportunity to learn to fill in empty time, nor to accumulate the various skills that would help them fill in time successfully.)

6. TV has a negative effect on children's physical fitness.
   (A scientific study finds a direct relationship between incidence of obesity among children and time spent watching TV.)

7. TV has a negative effect on school achievement.
   (Kids who watch a lot of TV have less time to read, to do homework, they stay up later and go to school tired—all these are partial explanations for the statistics that show that heavy TV watchers get lower scores on most achievement tests.)

8. Television watching may be a serious addiction.
   (There is an addictive aspect to TV viewing that is rarely taken seriously—and yet it may have destructive consequences for some vulnerable viewers.)

Why a TV Turn-Off

A collection of quotes from parents and children who have taken part in other TV Turn-Offs, demonstrating some of the ways a Turn-Off works to change lives:

An Opportunity to Discover New Activities

> The week I turned off my television I read more books, my school grades got a little better, I practiced piano more, I also learned to knit, I played a lot of indoor games with my sister and brothers, I got to know my family and myself better.
>
> —Sixth grader, Richmond, Indiana

> I found a lot of things to do (instead of watching TV): I read a lot of books. I invited some friends over to my house. I listened to the Super Bowl on the radio. I earned money by doing extra chores around the house. I finished practicing piano and violin, . . . I learned how to make carrot curls while my Mom was making dinner. I made a bird feeder.
>
> —Second grader, Farmington, Connecticut

> After a while I did get used to doing other things. The family started playing "Password" a lot. I also started exercising with a Richard Simmons record and I enjoy it. I'm glad now I was "encouraged" to cut down on TV. I can do more things than I used to. I'm reading more often and getting better at it too.
>
> —Eighth grader, Farmington, Connecticut

Educational Benefits in the Classroom

> During January, when Farmington turned off TV, I didn't notice big differences in individual children. However I did notice a difference in the class. The children were less tired, their play was less violent, and they were

better listeners. The children talked about many activities they had participated in with their families. Many more books were brought in for us to read because they were "good books Mom and Dad had read."

— Kindergarten teacher, Farmington, Connecticut

One day my class was getting ready to have a science test. It was Turn-Off Week. There was nothing to do so I studied instead. I studied all week. We did not have the test until Monday. I got S—. That is a good grade. When we had a History test I only missed 1 of 35. My grade was an E. My parents were proud of me. I was proud of myself too.

— Fourth grader, Marshall, Missouri

A Sense of Pride and Accomplishment

The most apparent result of becoming a family committed to Farmington's Turn-Off: the pride we all gained in being committed, of surviving (and even enjoying!) "doing without," of stretching ourselves in the pursuit of trying something new. . . . As a family we are proud of ourselves and of each other for having made this effort together—and for doing so well. Nothing we could have watched all month would have given us that.

— Parent, Farmington, Connecticut

More Family Closeness

Through the week it was kind of fun without the TV. It helped me get closer to my family. It also made me help my sister with something she was having trouble with.

— Third grader, Marshall, Missouri

Being a single parent who works two jobs, I hadn't realized that I was losing ground with my children. This week helped me realize that we needed to spend more time together and get to know each other. . . . My children and I have decided that there will be no TV in our house two nights a week. That will be our days to be a family. I think the Turn-Off was the best thing that has happened in Marshall.

—Mother, Marshall, Missouri

More Reading

Now that I couldn't watch TV I thought of other things to do.... I read all the books that I had classified as "boring" and discovered how good they really were.

—Sixth grader, Marshall, Missouri

More Time for Other Things

Every day when I came home from school I discovered that I had twice as much time to do things that I enjoyed: writing letters, playing outdoors, reading, working on my favorite subject, math, and hooking rugs. I also made an embroidered sample that my school librarian put on display!

—Sixth grader, Farmington, Connecticut

A New Understanding of TV's Role in Child-rearing

I didn't realize how much I use the TV to entertain the kids and keep them quiet. I was amazed at how creative the girls were when TV was not an option.

—Mother, Marshall, Missouri

We never realized before how automatic it was for us to turn on the TV.

—Parent, Buffalo, New York

I enjoyed my children a lot this week. I also found out how resourceful they are and it wasn't hard to keep them busy at all. I never realized how much TV we watch until I stopped and counted. We're going to enjoy doing without it more often.

—Parent, Marshall, Missouri

Long-lasting Effects on TV Habits

The TV no longer goes on automatically. A week without it seems to have broken the habit. We continue to spend more time doing things together.

—Parent, Marshall, Missouri

The Turn-Off was a super idea! Not only do we think before turning it on, but it does not occur to Ben (six) that the first thing to do is to watch TV. He plays much more with his toys.

—Parent, Buffalo, New York

What is most thrilling to us about this whole project is the fact that now, some three months later, the effect of it is still with us! The lasting effect on our children has been overwhelming! Not only do our children not watch TV now, except for special events, they don't even think about it! They now, especially the three-year-old, spend their time more creatively and actively. They have kicked the habit!

—Parent, Farmington, Connecticut

Selling a TV Turn-Off to Kids
[How to Encourage School-age Kids to Take Part in a Turn-Off]

1. It's a scientific experiment.
(The data collected in a Turn-Off will add to general understanding of TV's role.)

2. "We're all in this together."
(Turn-Off is not being inflicted on child "for your own good" but will challenge adults and children alike.)

3. The Turn-Off is a challenge.
(Can we survive a week without TV?)

4. It's something new and different.
(The Turn-Off is a break in the routine of daily life—will make life more interesting, though hard.)

5. It's not a punishment.
(This is different from the times that TV deprivation is used as a punishment—it will be more fun—and there's a reward at the end!)

6. The reward.
(The idea of a reward is more important than the actual reward chosen.)

Selling a TV Turn-Off to a Reluctant or Addicted Spouse

1. Don't assume he or she will say "no"—present the idea confidently and positively.

2. Emphasize the benefits of a Turn-Off for the children.

3. Think of a deal—"I'll go on a diet, if you cooperate in the Turn-Off," or something of the sort.

3. If spouse won't join, try for a show of solidarity in front of the children—this usually results in less viewing by the spouse, and may be the beginning of a change in viewing patterns.

Turn-Off Survival Hints for Families

The TV Turn-Off is at hand. You may be worrying about how your family will survive, especially on weekend mornings, without early-morning cartoons. Here are some hints that might help:

1. Plan More Social Activities for the Family

Invite friends over, especially other families participating in the Turn-Off. The more people around—for meals, for after-dinner games, for a weekend picnic—the better! Involve the kids in planning and cooking a special meal. Consider some group games that can be played by adults together with children of various ages—charades, Truth or Consequences, Twenty Questions, etc. Does anyone know any magic tricks? Could the kids be encouraged to put on a play or a skit?

2. Plan Social Life for Kids

Try to organize the children's social life during the day more than you usually do. Have the children invite friends over, and plan some special project for these visits in case the children are used to spending most of the time with their friends watching TV.

3. Read Aloud

Pick an exciting book with a lot of action, preferably one that can be left hanging at a suspenseful point each night. (See your classroom teacher or librarian for lists of good read-aloud books.) And don't forget to let older kids take their turn reading aloud.

4. Expand Your Family Horizons

Take this opportunity to think about new hobbies or family activities you've never had the time to pursue—stamp collecting, writing to pen pals, keeping a family scrapbook, starting a family genealogy, sewing or arts and crafts projects, and so on.

5. Write Letters

Writing letters is a great lesson in deferred gratification: it takes a bit of time and effort to write a letter, address it, mail it. Then more time passes. And then . . . jackpot! A letter in return arrives in the mail. During a Turn-Off the time for such leisurely occupations as letter-writing is suddenly available—not *required* letters such as thank-you notes, but letters that promise exciting answers, such as fan letters to a favorite author or actress or baseball player.

6. *Stock up on Equipment*

Stock up on basic equipment—art materials, games, puzzles, etc. This is the time to get things out of the closet or attic that were put away years ago—old toys or games, appliances or tools that no one has used for a long time. Old family photograph albums are particularly fascinating to most children and can fill up many happy hours for those with time on their hands. Older children are often amazingly interested in their "baby toys," put away years ago, and will actually play with their old blocks or Legos or dolls, sometimes for hours.

7. *Plan Ahead for Saturday Morning*

For the Saturday-morning-without-cartoons-blues: Try preparing some special project or leaving out a special game or activity on Friday night for the kids to find when they wake up Saturday morning . . . maybe they'll even let you sleep!

8. *Get Outdoors*

All outdoor sports—organized games such as baseball, soccer, or basketball, biking, skating, running, or just plain walking—are especially suitable for filling in free time during a Turn-Off, if for no other reason than to make everyone deliciously tired at bedtime (which, many families report, comes considerably earlier in the absence of evening TV programs).

9. *Take Special Trips*

The Turn-Off is a good time for special trips—to museums, to police stations and firehouses, to the local courthouse—wherever: you now have a fine spur to undertake all those interesting trips you have always planned but never quite got around to taking.

10. *Use the Radio and Stereo*

Educators and child experts have begun to discover advantages in radio listening that do not apply to television viewing. For example, listening to the radio helps develop reading skills, for when children listen to the radio, they are obliged to create their own mental pictures to go along with the sounds. This is not unlike the mental activity required to transform written words on a page into a meaningful story in a child's mind.

For this reason the radio should not be overlooked as a valuable resource during a TV Turn-Off. Indeed, rediscovering the radio may be one of the important benefits of a TV Turn-Off.

There are also records that may help make the unfilled hours of a Turn-Off more delightful—recordings of famous authors reading children's classics, for instance, as well as records of musicals, Gilbert and Sullivan operettas, comedy routines, old radio programs like "The Shadow" or "The Green Hornet," etc., any of which might be the beginning of a lifetime of new interests.

11. Self-Improvement Projects

With hours of extra time on everyone's hands, a Turn-Off is a fine time for a variety of self-improvement projects: anything from exercise and calisthenics regimes to practicing a musical instrument or learning a foreign language. Besides self-improvement, there are related areas that may need improvement too—clothes that need mending, drawers or closets that need cleaning out, and so on. And for kids, of course, there's always homework that needs doing more thoroughly, writing projects to get a start on. Finally, there is always Christmas or Hanukkah to start planning for, even many months in advance.

12. Humanitarian Activities

The extra hours provided by the TV Turn-Off are well suited to worthy programs that many families would like to be involved in but often feel they simply haven't the spare time for. This is the week to spend more time at church- or synagogue-related service projects, helping in a program for the homeless, for instance, or sorting used clothes for distribution to the needy. Children, it should be noted, also seem more willing to go to Sunday school or choir practice during a TV Turn-Off, when they feel they are not missing their usual Sunday morning programs.

15. *Relax!*

Don't feel obliged to entertain your kids yourselves as a substitute for the TV set. Part of the purpose of this experiment is to let you see how resourceful your kids really are and can be, if there is no TV to keep them occupied. Don't feel everybody has to fill in every minute of time doing something creative, or worthy, or educational. Give everybody in the family a chance to experience unstructured time—empty time—time to do nothing at all, and see what happens. Sometimes the most important impulses or plans or ideas are born at times like these.

Basic Art Recipes for Home Play
(for one or two children)

Watercolor Paint

Dilute food coloring with water and put in small glasses. Use as paint with brushes or Q-tips or eraser end of pencil.

Paper Paste

⅓ cup flour
2 tablespoons sugar
1 cup water
¼ teaspoon oil of peppermint or wintergreen (optional)
saucepan

Mix flour and sugar. Gradually add water. Stir well. Cook over low heat stirring constantly, until clear. Remove from heat and add oil. Store in a jar. Will last a few weeks.

Can be used in making collages.

Play Clay

½ cup salt
½ cup hot water
¼ cup cold water
½ cup cornstarch
saucepan

1. Mix salt and hot water in pan and bring to boil.
2. Stir cornstarch into cold water and add to boiling mixture.
3. Stir vigorously and cook over low heat until stiff.
4. Remove from heat, let cool, and knead until smooth and pliable.

Store in airtight container to keep soft. After forming into shapes, animals, etc., either let dry for one or two days and then paint, or bake at 200° for one hour and paint.

Play Dough

2 cups unsifted flour
1 cup salt
1 cup (or less) of water with food coloring
2 tablespoons cooking oil

Combine ingredients in a mixing bowl and mix thoroughly. Then, knead ingredients together until consistency of dough.

Homemade Fingerpaints

½ cup *instant* cold-water starch
½ cup soap flakes (not powder or detergent)
5 ounces water

Beat ingredients together until they are consistency of whipped potatoes. Add food coloring for vibrant color.

How to fingerpaint:
Child can paint directly on Formica-topped or plastic table, on a plastic tray or on an aluminum cookie sheet. Or you can buy fingerpaint paper.

1. Moisten table, tray, or paper with damp sponge.
2. Put about a spoonful of paint on surface.
3. Let the child coat the area with open palm until the paint on the hand is used up.
4. Add another spoonful, and then another, until the entire painting surface is coated.
5. Child then makes picture by rubbing fingers (or hands or arms) in paint, leaving a design.
6. If child doesn't like the design, it can be "erased" by recoating the surface.

Vegetable Printing

(Potatoes work best, but you can use carrots, turnips, etc.)

1. Cut vegetable to give you a flat surface.
2. Draw a simple design on it—a star, triangle, moon, or other simple shape.

3. You can either hollow out the design or cut down the vegetable around it, leaving the design raised. (Adult does the carving.)
4. Blot vegetable on paper towel.
5. Paint the raised part with poster paint and brush.
6. Print the design on paper or fabric.

Straw Printing

> Watered poster paints
> A drinking straw for each child
> Paper for painting

1. Pour about a tablespoon of paint in the middle of each child's paper.
2. Child directs paint all over paper by blowing a stream of air at it through a straw.

(Straw should be held about an inch above the paper. It should not touch the paint. If children insist on trying to drink the paint, forget about this kind of painting.)

B. Nuts and Bolts: Everything You Need for a Family, Classroom, Early Childhood, and School TV Turn-Off

Family Viewing Chart

(Please write in name of program, and how long it was watched, for every family member.)

MONDAY
morning   afternoon   evening

TUESDAY
morning   afternoon   evening

WEDNESDAY
morning   afternoon   evening

THURSDAY
morning   afternoon   evening

FRIDAY
morning   afternoon   evening

SATURDAY
morning   afternoon   evening

SUNDAY
morning   afternoon   evening

The TV Turn-Off Battle Plan for (name): _____

MONDAY
afternoon, after school:

evening, after dinner:

TUESDAY
afternoon, after school:

evening, after dinner:

WEDNESDAY
afternoon, after school:

evening, after dinner:

THURSDAY
afternoon, after school:

evening, after dinner:

FRIDAY
afternoon, after school:

evening, after dinner:

Weekend Battle Plan

SATURDAY
morning

afternoon

evening

SUNDAY
morning

afternoon

evening

Letter to Kids Taking Part in a TV Turn-Off

You are about to take part in an exciting experiment that parents and kids all over the country will be interested in hearing about: you are going to try to spend a whole week without watching any TV. You will learn some surprising things about television during this week—how different life is without TV available to fill in your free time, and what different things you do when TV isn't available to watch. But it may be harder than you think! So here are some ideas that might help you fill in the time you usually spend watching TV.

1. READ: Go to your school library or to the public library and take out a whole pile of books.

2. BE A COOK: Make cookies or cake or candy. Or cook a whole dinner for your family.

3. ORGANIZE: Rearrange your room, your closet, your clothes drawer.

4. GET IN SHAPE: Start on an exercise program. Jog a mile. See how many push-ups or sit-ups you can do.

5. BE A GARDENER: Plant seeds from various foods. Try orange seeds or lemon seeds. Plant carrot tops or pineapple tops. Plant a potato eye.

6. BE AN ARTIST: Make a collage out of magazine and newspaper clippings, candy wrappers, or anything else you find around. Make ornaments for next Christmas out of baking clay. (See recipe for Play Clay on page 164.)

7. INVENT A GAME: Make up a board game or a new card game. Make up a word search game with the names of your family and friends in it. Try these out on your parents or friends.

8. SEND AWAY FOR THINGS: Send for free things with coupons from newspapers or magazines. You'll get a lot of mail!

9. MAKE PLANS FOR THE FUTURE: What would you do if you had a million dollars? If you could be president? If you could go anywhere in the world? If you could be some other person, who would you pick? Why?

10. BE A WRITER: Write a story, poem, or play and send it to a magazine that prints kids' writings. Write a letter to the editors of a newspaper and give a kid's point of view on some news story. (They love to print letters from kids if they are short and clearly

written!) Write a fan letter to a favorite author and send it to her or him c/o the publisher of the book. (Most authors will write back!)

OTHER IDEAS OF GREAT THINGS TO DO:
(Send in three great ideas for future editions of this book.)

1.

2.

3.

Good luck! Even though TV watching can be lots of fun, don't forget that kids lived without TV for hundreds, for thousands of years and still managed to have fun. You might be surprised how much time you have to do things when you don't have TV to simply turn on when you have nothing to do. Some of the things you do during No-TV Week might be more fun than you imagine . . . and you might never have tried them if you hadn't turned off the TV set!

The Turn-Off Diary

For most children, the ideal Turn-Off diary is a small spiral memo notebook (approximately 3 inches by 5 inches) with a 36-inch shoelace attached to the spiral binding so that it may be worn around the neck. Wearing the diary during the Turn-Off not only adds an intriguing touch to a child's everyday appearance but also makes the diary easily available at the moment a thought comes to mind, or a new activity is embarked upon. For families with young children, a single "Family Turn-Off Diary" is suitable, which the children can help decorate, and into which they can dictate their thoughts and ideas. For older children—third graders and up—each member of the family does best with his or her own diary.

The No-TV Button

For participants in all Turn-Offs, whether family or school centered, having a "real" No-TV button to wear during the week is vital. If you can borrow or buy a button-making machine (see below for ordering instructions—allow three to four weeks for delivery), then all family members can make their own designs and end up with a professional-looking button to wear during the No-TV period. Or you may buy ready-made buttons of TV stars and convert them into No-TV buttons by drawing a diagonal slash across them with an indelible marker.

For younger children, a simple button made out of cardboard and a safety pin, which they can help make is probably more satisfying than one that is ready-made.

You can order a simple machine for creating buttons, and all the materials necessary, from:
Badge-a-Minit
348 N. 30th Rd.
Box 800, La Salle, IL 61301

A starter kit costs $26.95, which includes materials to make ten buttons. You can order larger quantities of button parts, costing from $9.95 for 50, to $129.95 for 1,000. There is a catalog that describes a variety of machines available.

No-TV Week Contract—Early Childhood
(To Be Read to Younger Children)

I _____

HEREBY AGREE TO THE FOLLOWING CONDITIONS:

1. That I will not watch TV for an entire week.

2. That during those times when I usually watch television, I will try very hard to do other things. Also we will spend time reading aloud each day.

3. That I will keep a diary, or help someone in my family keep a diary by telling them all the special things I did during the Turn-Off Week, and also all my feelings about not watching TV.

The Turn-Off will last from _____ to _____.

This contract will be in force all those days.

I also agree that by signing this contract, and spending one whole week without watching TV, I will be entitled to a reward that everybody will agree upon before the Turn-Off begins.

Signed _____

(Affix seal here)

(For schools)
Parent's permission:

I understand the purpose of the TV Turn-Off and agree to my child's participation. I will try to help him/her do other things during the Turn-Off period.

Parent's signature_____

Please return by_____
(date)

No-TV Week Contract—
(Grades 3 to 6)

KNOW YE, ALL MEN, WOMEN, AND CHILDREN—
BY THIS CONTRACT FOR FULL AND DUE CONSIDERATION,
THAT:

Name_____(Please print)

HEREBY AGREES TO ALL TERMS AND CONDITIONS SET FORTH
BELOW:

1. That he/she shall not view television for one entire week or engage in any television-related activity (such as playing video games or watching VCRs.)
2. That he/she will make a positive effort to engage in other activities, games, projects, get-togethers with friends, and sundry enterprises during those times said individual might otherwise be watching television, and not just spend that time weeping and bewailing the loss of that familiar and usual occupation (television watching).
3. That said individual (the above-named) will maintain a careful diary during the Turn-Off period, containing a detailed record of all activities, projects, games, get-togethers, and sundry activities that have taken the place of television watching during No-TV Week, as well as an honest record of all occasions when temptation to watch was not resisted, along with an honest record of all good and bad feelings about the absence of television during this Turn-Off.

THE PERIOD OF THIS CONTRACT SHALL BE FROM _____
(date of beginning) THROUGH _____ (date of ending)
INCLUSIVE (a period of at least one week).

UPON THE SATISFACTORY COMPLETION OF THIS CONTRACT
THE ABOVE-NAMED PARTY SHALL THEN BE ENTITLED TO A
SPECIAL REWARD THAT HAD BEEN DETERMINED BY MUTUAL
CONSENT PRIOR TO THE NO-TV PERIOD.

(affix seal here)

Signature _____

The Kick-off Ceremony
for Families at Home

1. The family gathers around the television set. With great seriousness (and an equal sense of fun), each person bids a formal farewell to television watching for a week. (This may take the form of a little speech, incantation, song [dirge] or a simple good-bye.) Affectionate hugs and kisses, or "pats on the back," are bestowed upon the soon-to-be darkened machine.

2. The contracts are brought out and a seal of some sort is now attached, making them "legally" binding.

3. A pre-selected person now ceremoniously unplugs the television set from the wall outlet.

4. Finally, with as much ceremony (and fun) as possible, a funeral shroud (blanket, sheet, etc.) is draped over each set in the house, to remain in place for the duration of the Turn-Off. (Since television watching is so often done out of sheer habit, this covering of the sets acts as a reminder to all that a Turn-Off is in progress, thus preventing accidental breaches of contract.)

5. If there is time, the Kick-off Ceremony may conclude with a reading of some favorite cautionary writings about television, such as Shel Silverstein's famous poem about Jimmy Jet and His TV Set, or Roald Dahl's anti-TV poem from *Charlie and the Chocolate Factory*.

The Kick-off Ceremony for the Classroom

You may not have a TV set in your classrom, and so the solemn farewells that mark the beginning of the Kick-off Ceremony may be made to any symbolic TV, even a picture of a TV set. Or you may have some artistic children in the class construct a fantastic TV reproduction out of a cardboard carton, wires, buttons, etc.

1. A selected child goes to the front of the room and solemnly unplugs the TV set or its facsimile.

2. A second child steps up and shrouds the TV set with a piece of dark cloth.

3. One by one the kids in the class file by the set to say their last farewells. Each child tells what program he will miss the most, and what activities he will do instead of TV viewing.

4. Speeches, poems, and dramatic readings are now in order.

5. Each child now signs a contract. A seal or gold star is affixed thereon.

6. Diaries and No-TV buttons are distributed.

The Turn-Off has officially begun!

A Sample Notice for a Parents' Meeting about Television

* * *   IMPORTANT NOTICE FOR ALL PARENTS   * * *

Dear Parents:

Making the right decisions about television is crucial to your child's educational future, as well as to your future as a family. Now, when your children are young, is the time to establish the best viewing patterns.

Please come to an important meeting about television on (date and time) at (place of meeting).

We will present information about television's impact on children's school achievement and we would like to hear your own concerns about television.

Before you leave we will propose that you take part in an experiment that will help you understand how television is affecting your child's development and the way your family spends time together.

I hope you will take the time to attend this important meeting. Child care will be provided.

(Your signature) _____

Please check one:

_____ I can come to the meeting.

_____ I cannot come.

(Signature _____)

How to Organize and Run
a Parents' Meeting about Television

Hints

The tone of your presentation is crucial; a "We're all in this together" attitude is more persuasive than a "I'm here to help you see the light" approach. It is important to emphasize from the start that the purpose of the Turn-Off is not to make parents feel guilty about their use of TV, but to help them gain better control over it in their homes.

The Parents' Meeting is not the occasion for a general consideration of the good and bad sides of television—or any debate about program content. The focus at such a meeting must be the negative impact of excessive viewing on children's development and educational achievement, as well as the promotion of alternative activities to television watching, foremost among them reading.

Organizational Outline

1. Welcome parents—start with coffee, cookies, or other refreshments if possible.

2. Encourage parents to exchange experiences about television problems, steering the discussion away from programs and toward the excessive use of TV.

3. From your vantage point as educator, briefly describe some of the negative effects of excessive TV viewing. (See chapter 1 for specific areas of concern; or use "What's Wrong with Watching TV?" on page 154 as a reference.)

4. Explain the purpose of a TV Turn-Off. For an Early Childhood Turn-Off, stress that early childhood is the ideal time to work on establishing good television viewing patterns in the family—*before* bad patterns need to be undone.

5. Point out that a common reaction to the Turn-Off idea—"Oh, I couldn't survive a week without TV!"—is an important warning sign of a potentially serious TV problem within the family.

6. Finally, have parents sign up for participation in the Turn-Off. Try for 100 percent class participation, asking parents to make calls to those families who did not attend the meeting. Be sure parents include a telephone number.

A Follow-up Letter after Early Childhood
Parents' Meeting about Television

Dear Parents:

As you may have heard, our class will soon be involved in an unusual experiment—a TV Turn-Off. During the week of (_____) participating families will test their survival skills by going "cold turkey" from all television viewing.

The purpose of a TV Turn-Off is not to attack television or make people feel guilty about watching it. It is to help parents and children get a better idea of how television affects their lives. It is a great opportunity for your family to discover if television is having a greater influence on your children's development, on their play, and on the quality of your family life than you imagine. Most important, since excessive television viewing can have an adverse effect on your child's future school achievement, now is the time to take steps to gain control over this very attractive and sometimes addictive medium. A TV Turn-Off can help your family begin to establish such control before unfavorable viewing habits have a chance to develop.

Before the Turn-Off, you will receive some pages with suggested activities to help make the Turn-Off an adventure rather than a deprivation for your child. You will also receive some suggestions for strategies to make the Turn-Off easier for you as a parent to manage. There will be a contract and a special Turn-Off button for all participants to wear, a kick-off ceremony, and a party at the end—in short, some fun along with something that may also be difficult.

I am hoping that every parent in my class will participate in this important experiment.

(Signature) _____

A Follow-up Letter to Parents
Involved in a Classroom TV Turn-Off

Dear Parents:

As you may have heard, our class is taking part in a week-long experiment, a TV Turn-Off. Everyone in the class—children and teachers—will be asked to sign a contract pledging that they will not watch any form of TV for the period of an entire week. They will be encouraged to get involved with new activities—especially reading—and to keep a careful diary of all the changes they observe during the TV Turn-Off.

The purpose of a TV Turn-Off is not to attack television. It is to help children and families get a better understanding of the role TV plays in their lives. It is a great opportunity for your child, and perhaps your whole family, to discover if television watching might be having a greater influence than you imagine on your children's use of free time, on reading, on playing, on learning, on conversations, on mealtimes—in short, on the quality of family life.

During the week before the Turn-Off, the children will be involved in various classroom activities related to television viewing. The following week will be the TV Turn-Off. At the end of the experiment we will have a party to celebrate our successful completion of the Turn-Off.

I know you will be hearing more about our TV Turn-Off from your child. I hope your whole family will consider taking part in this experiment. But if that is not possible, I hope you will encourage your child to accept the challenge and spend this one special week doing other things besides watching TV, and I hope you will help your child in this worthy project by scheduling some special family activities during the Turn-Off week.

Sincerely,

(Classroom teacher's signature)

Spanish Translation of Follow-up Letter to Parents

Queridos padres,

Como ustedes sabrán, la clase de su hijo/hija está participando en un experimento que tendrá lugar la semana que viene—SEMANA SIN TELEVISIÓN.

El objeto de est experimento es ayudar a los niños y a sus padres comprender el papel que la televisión tiene en sus vidas. Es una magnífica oportunidad para ustedes y sus hijos para descubrir si la televisión tiene mayor influencia que ustedes sospechaban en la manera que sus hijos utilizan tiempo libre, hacen lectura, manera de jugar, conversación, comidas familiares—en fin, sobre la calidad de la vida familial.

Esta semana, los muchachos harán varios ejercicios en sus clases analizando la televisión. La semana que viene, desde el (la fecha) hasta el (la fecha) se celebrara la SEMANA SIN TELEVISIÓN. (La fecha) habrá una fiesta para todos los que participaron en la SEMANA SIN TELEVISIÓN.

Yo sé que sus hijos les hablarán de la SEMANA SIN TELEVI-SIÓN. Espero que tendran interés en participar con su familia. Pero, si eso no es posible, espero que ayudará a sus hijos participar en este experimento y que les ofrecerán actividades que no sean ver televisión.

Sinceramente,

_____

Activities and Assignments for Pre-Turn-Off Week (Grades 3–6)

• *Assign an interview with someone who grew up before the advent of television.* What did they do in their free time? What were some family activities? Do they watch TV now? How do they feel about it? Do they think they would have had more fun if they had had TV at home when they were children?

• *Writing assignment:* Hold an imaginary conversation with children your age from some other country (or planet) who have never seen or heard about TV. Try to explain and describe TV to them—what you like about it, what you don't like. Try to imagine what kinds of things they do in their country (or planet) during their free time—you can invent any kind of weird activity!

• *Writing assignment or a class discussion about family attitudes toward TV:* How do your parents feel about your television watching? Do they think you watch too much? Do they like or dislike the programs you watch? What about your parents' TV watching? Do they ever watch TV when you wish they would talk with you or play with you? Do you have any rules about TV at home? When do you watch the most TV? What are some possible alternative activities that would make you want to skip your favorite programs?

• *Writing assignment—to do in class toward the end of the Turn-Off:* What are your feelings about No-TV Week? Have you learned anything about how TV affects your life?

• *Using statistics from the viewing charts, there are many kinds of graphs your class can make which will cast new light on each child's viewing habits.* A bar graph, for instance, can make it immediately clear to each child whether his or her daily consumption of TV is more or less than the average. Making graphs is a valuable math exercise as well. Below are examples of the different kinds of graphs that have been made in different Classroom Turn-Offs throughout the country:

• *For School Turn-Offs:* Work on an essay for the essay contest.

Note to teachers: You will probably come up with a number of other assignments or activities suitable to the pre-Turn-Off period. Please share these with readers of future editions of this book. See Author's Note, page 198, for details on writing in.

Follow-up Questionnaire

A very important part of a Turn-Off experiment is to hear from parents about their observations and impressions of their children's behavior and activities during the No-TV period, as well as their impressions of the effect of a Turn-Off on the whole family.

Would you please fill out the brief questionnaire below, and add your comments about how the Turn-Off affected your children and your family life.

Child's name _____

Classroom teacher _____

Did your entire family participate in the Turn-Off? _____

How many TV sets in your home _____

Is there a TV set in your child's room? _____

Does your family watch TV during dinner?   Sometimes _____

Often _____

Almost never _____

About how many hours of TV does your child watch each week?

Total hours _____

How many hours do parents watch?

Total hours _____

Do you limit the amount of time your child watches TV?

Yes _____

I try, but I don't generally succeed _____

Do you limit the kinds of programs your child watches? Explain:

Follow-up Questionnaire (continued)

Comments about the Turn-Off: (Please be as specific as possible about any changes you observed, and the new activities your child and family did during the Turn-Off. Please mention whether more time was spent on homework and reading):

Has the Turn-Off brought about any changes in your family TV use? Please explain:

Follow-up Letter to Teachers about a School TV Turn-Off

Re: The TV Turn-Off
To: Teachers at (school) ——
From:

Dear Colleagues:

As you know, during the week of ——————— to ———————,
the school community is taking part in a TV Turn-Off, an experiment that asks participants to turn off television entirely for a
period of a week.

The purpose of a Turn-Off is not to attack television: it is to help
teachers, parents, and children better understand the role that television plays in their daily lives, by allowing them to observe the
changes that occur when TV is not available.

Since television plays so crucial a part in children's lives today,
and since its effects are being observed by teachers in every classroom, this is a unique opportunity for you to begin to consider
with your class some of the ways TV may be affecting their family
life, their use of free time, their schoolwork, and so on.

I would strongly like to encourage you to consider classroom
involvement in the Turn-Off. While the Turn-Off must necessarily
be a volunteer activity, your interest might help your entire class
decide to participate. With full participation, a Turn-Off becomes
an exciting and unforgettable project—one that brings the class
together in a new way.

The week immediately preceding the Turn-Off (from Monday,
—— to Friday,——) has been set aside for pre-Turn-Off activities.
A list of possible activities will be sent to all teachers outlining
some of the ways other schools have utilized a Turn-Off for the
best educational purposes.

Yours sincerely,

(Signature) ————————————

A Model Invitation for Recognition Day

YOU SURVIVED THE TURN-OFF—
AND NOW FOR THE REWARD
PLEASE COME TO OUR
RECOGNITION DAY PARTY

Where:
When:

PRIZES ★ ENTERTAINMENT ★
★ REFRESHMENTS ★

_____

Readings from Turn-Off Diaries
Sharing the Experience

Organization of Recognition Night Party

7:00–7:30. Set up refreshments, prizes, certificates, prepare microphones for speakers, have extra chairs ready for overflow crowd. (Since whole families who participated are invited to Recognition Day, there may be a real crowd attending.)

7:30. People arrive

7:30–7:50. Kids pick up prizes

7:50–8:30. Kids, parents, and teachers speak about their Turn-Off experiences (a list of speakers has been prepared beforehand)

8:30–8:50. Skits, poems, entertainment

8:50–9:15. Refreshments

9:15–9:30. Organizer gives out certificates, says final words, acknowledges help from various parents and teachers

9:30. Party is over

Special Activities for Public Libraries
to Organize during a Large-scale Turn-Off

1. Schedule extra programs for children—evening story hours, film showings, special speakers.

2. Plan extra programs for adults—hobby and craft demonstrations, book-discussion programs

3. Plan a special Read-Aloud Hour to be held every day at a regular hour during the Turn-Off. This can take the place of after-school TV viewing for many children. You might have two stories available, one for young children, another for older schoolchildren.

4. Acquire board games and other family-type activities that Turn-Off participants may borrow in the same way they borrow books during the Turn-Off.

5. Have a Turn-Off Hotline—a special number people can call for help in filling in their time during a Turn-Off.

6. Have a Homework Clinic available, with teenage volunteers willing to work with kids on homework problems. Make this seem like fun by including refreshments.

7. Have displays of especially exciting books available for borrowing and bill them as GREAT TURN-OFF TIME-FILLERS—reading these books will be more fun than watching television!

The Certificate of Merit

CERTIFICATE OF MERIT

This is to Certify that

_____

(name)

successfully completed a week-long
TV TURN-OFF,
and discovered not only
that there definitely
IS
 LIFE WITHOUT TV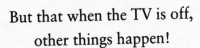

But that when the TV is off,
other things happen!

The Pledge Card
THE SCHOOL
TELEVISION TURN-OFF PLEDGE CARD

NAME _____ GRADE _____

ADDRESS _____ PHONE _____

TEACHER _____

I PLEDGE TO TURN OFF MY TV FOR THE ENTIRE WEEK OF

SIGNATURE _____

(check one)
____ My entire family is going "cold turkey" with me
____ I am doing the Turn-Off on my own

Child's Signature _____

Parent's Signature _____

Return this card by (Month and date) to (Teacher) or (Librarian)

THE SCHOOL TURN-OFF
VERIFICATION CARD

NAME _____ GRADE _____

ADDRESS _____ PHONE _____

TEACHER _____

____ I went "cold turkey" for the entire week

____ I cut down to ____ hours for the entire week

____ My entire family went "cold turkey"

Signature _____

Parent's signature _____

Return this card by (Month and date) to (Teacher) or (Librarian)

The pledge card contains two halves, with a perforated line separating them. The top half is the pledge to "turn off TV" during the No-TV period, to be handed in before the Turn-Off. The lower half is the verification, on which the participants can note how well they succeeded during the Turn-Off. This is to be handed in at the Recognition Day party, or to a classroom teacher at a later date.

Sample Press Release—School TV Turn-Off

Date

For Immediate Release:

*****THE GREAT TV TURN-OFF AT THE ANYTOWN SCHOOL*****

From _____ to _____ a TV Turn-Off will be conducted at (name of school). During this week, participating classes, teachers, and entire families will turn off television sets entirely in order to gain a new understanding of the role TV plays in children's and family life, as well as to observe the effect of its temporary absence on school achievement.

During the week before the Turn-Off participating classes will engage in special educational activities related to television. During the No-TV period, all those who have signed contracts to go "cold turkey" will wear identifying No-TV buttons, and keep a diary of the changes that occur in their lives as a consequence of turning off the TV.

Students, parents, and teachers will be available during the entire Turn-Off period for interview by appointment. An especially good time for coverage of this unusual event will be Recognition Day, on (date), at (time) and (place), at which parents, teachers, and children will tell of their No-TV experiences and read from their diaries. Prizes and recognition certificates will be distributed.

For further information contact: (name of organizer)
(telephone)

or (name of principal)
(telephone)

Sample Press Releases for Large-scale TV Turn-Offs

For immediate release:

* * * THE GREAT TV TURN-OFF * * *
* * * COMMUNITY GOES COLD TURKEY * * *

During the week of (dates) the entire community of _____ is invited to take part in "The Great TV Turn-Off" by pledging to go "cold turkey" and not watch television for an entire week.

(Name of organizer) and (names of others involved), parents, are coordinating this program with the (name of community) Library system, in order to promote reading and other family activities during Children's Book Week, (month and dates).

This project was generated by the growing concern of parents and educators that children are spending too much of their leisure time watching television, replacing such activities as reading, conversation, and various forms of play.

The Great TV Turn-Off has drawn widespread support throughout the community, with cultural organizations such as _____ and businesses such as _____ joining in as official supporters.

An information meeting for parents will be held at (place and address) on (date) at (time) A panel, including a child psychologist, a librarian, and a parent who has removed TV from her home, will discuss this issue and offer advice to families taking part in The Great TV Turn-Off.

For more information, contact (name and phone number of organizer).

or (name and phone number of assistant)

194 ·

* * *   TURN OFF TV FOR A WEEK!   * * *
FOR IMMEDIATE RELEASE

Librarians and educators are challenging area residents to join a Community TV Turn-Off from (dates) and spend a week without television. Participants will be asked to sign a Cold Turkey Pledge to turn off TV during that week.

"If participants in the Turn-Off can go one week without television," states project director (name and title), "they are likely to discover many enjoyable alternatives to TV and become more selective and controlled in their future viewing." (name of organizer) believes that there is good cause for concern about excessive TV viewing: According to the A. C. Nielsen Co., the national average of family viewing time in 1983 was 7.02 hours per day.

(number of other libraries participating) school librarians will participate in the Turn-Off and will act as coordinators of their individual school activities during the Turn Off TV campaign. The (name of library council, or affiliate of larger reading association, such as IRA, etc.), as well as a number of other community agencies and organizations, have pledged their support of the Turn Off TV project.

Residents of (name of community) who turn off TV for the entire week will receive a certificate to be awarded at Recognition Day at (place and time). The program will feature (relevant details).

Any person interested in signing a pledge card may participate. Pledge cards will be available at (name of library or center of organization) in the area schools, and in other selected sites beginning (date).

For further information, contact: (name and phone number of organizers).

Sample Proclamation and Resolution

A Proclamation by the Mayor of Richmond, Indiana:

***Whereas libraries have been the storehouses of literature, knowledge, and culture since ancient times; and

***Whereas the books and manuscripts these libraries have held have captured and broadened the readers' imaginations for centuries; and

***Whereas reading is an alternative to television as a source of entertainment and bears all the advantages mentioned above; ***Now therefore, I, Frank H. Walterman, Mayor of the city of Richmond, do hereby declare November 12–18, 1984

Book Week and TV Turn-Off Week in the City of Roses and encourage all her citizens to read at least one book this week and every week they are able

***In witness thereof I have hereunto set my hand and caused the Seal of the City of Richmond, State of Indiana to be affixed this Third day of October, 1984

Resolution of the Board of School Trustees— Richmond Community Schools—September 24, 1984

***Whereas Morrison Reeves Library and Richmond Community Schools are promoting a week without television during Children's Book Week, November 12–18, 1984, and

***Whereas the Board of School Trustees shares the concern of Library Media Specialists and Educators that the excessive amount of television viewing may be a detriment to creativity and the educational growth of children and

***Whereas the Board of School Trustees supports the promotion of alternatives to watching TV, which include reading and a variety of activities sponsored by local institutions,

***We hereby endorse the "Turn Off TV" campaign to be held during Children's Book Week, November 12–18, 1984

Enlisting Community Support

PLEASE JOIN OUR TV TURN-OFF!!!
WE NEED YOUR HELP!!!

WHAT'S HAPPENING?
School (name) in cooperation with the Board of Education is sponsoring THE TV TURN-OFF during the week of (date).

WHAT'S THAT?
Our school community (and friends and families) will be encouraged to sign contracts and commit themselves to drastically reducing TV viewing during the Turn-Off week, or to go "cold turkey" from TV altogether! On (date), officially designated as Recognition Day, there will be a meeting/party for all participants in the Turn-Off with entertainment and prizes.

WHY?
The purpose of the Turn-Off is not to make people hate television and get rid of it forever. It is to make families more aware of the role TV plays in their lives. By turning off TV for a week, we hope people will be "turned on" by alternative activities—talking to each other, playing games, visiting friends, and reading—and will begin to control their viewing better in the future.

WHAT CAN OUR GROUP DO?
We want to invite you to be official supporters and participants in our Turn-Off. Members of your group can help plan special activities during the Turn-Off Week that will take the place of viewing. They can design posters and otherwise help spread the word of the event to the community at large.

WHEN?
Come to a planning meeting on (date, time and place).

WHAT'S IN IT FOR US?
Helping a worthy project, for one thing. Publicity for your group, for another. (There is sure to be some media attention paid to the Turn-Off—NO-TV is always news!) And finally, fun—in preparing a performance, or in coming to a great party, or in many other ways we can't even imagine yet.

SO JOIN IN WITH US
AND BECOME PART OF OUR TV TURN-OFF!

For more details, please call
(name and phone number of organizer)

A Model Letter to Merchants and Businesses

THE SCHOOL TV TURN-OFF:
WHAT IT IS AND WHY YOU SHOULD SUPPORT IT

Dear (town merchant or businessperson):

Did you know that television watching takes up more hours of the average child's life than any other activity, including school! While television's potential as a positive force is known, we as educators and parents are concerned about its adverse effects on school achievement and on family well-being.

In order to make families more aware of the role TV plays in their lives, our school is holding a TV Turn-Off during the week of (date). We are encouraging children and families to sign contracts and commit themselves to drastically reducing TV viewing during the Turn-Off week, or to go "cold turkey" from TV altogether! During the Turn-Off, teachers will conduct TV awareness activities in their classrooms. Other groups are planning family-centered activities to take the place of TV watching that week. On (date), officially designated as Recognition Day, there will be a meeting/party for all participants in the Turn-Off. There will be entertainment, people will have a chance to tell what they learned during the week of No TV, and all participants will receive a special prize.

We are soliciting your support in this important endeavor. You can help in any or all of the following ways:

1. We need contributions to help cover expenses connected with the Turn-Off—buying special No-TV buttons for all participants to wear, printing the pledge cards, poster materials, etc.

2. We need prizes to distribute on Recognition Day to all children who went "cold turkey"—children's books, educational toys, passes to cultural or sports events, etc.

(optional—for large-scale Turn-Off)

3. We need local merchants to contribute to a discount coupon booklet, which will be distributed to all who sign pledge cards. The coupons may be redeemed only during the week of the Turn-Off. While the purpose is to attract people to join the Turn-Off, there is an obvious trade-off for the merchant or business as well—attracting new customers, who may buy other things, and creating a lot of goodwill!

Please join in! We need your help!

signed   (organizer of Turn-Off)_____

Phone number _____

Author's Note

For inclusion in future editions of *Unplugging the Plug-in Drug,* please send your name, address, and information about your TV Turn-Off, and suggested activities to:

> Marie Winn
> c/o Viking Penguin Inc.
> 40 West 23rd Street
> New York, N.Y. 10010

TV Turn-Off Honor Roll

New York City, P.S. 166, No-TV Week—April 1977. Organizer: Marie Winn.

New York City, P.S. 84, No-TV Week—April 1985. Organizer: Marie Winn.

Hardwick, Vermont, Hazen Union School Turn-Off—November 1984.

Farmington, Connecticut, One month TV Turn-Off—January 1984; January 1985. Organizer: Nancy DeSalvo.

Buffalo, New York, School 54's Great TV Turn-Off—November 12–19, 1985. Organizer: Sandra Pezzino.

Richmond, Indiana, Turn-Off TV—Bring on the Books (held during Book Week) November 12–18, 1985. Organizer: Sue Weller.

Piscataway, New Jersey, Turn-Off the TV Month—April 1985. Organizers: Jane Kucharski and Robin del Giudice.

Marshall, Missouri, TV Turn-Off Week—March 6–13, 1986. Organizer: Martha Thornton.

[This is a partial list of some of the School or Community TV Turn-Offs that have come to my attention. I know there have been many more. If you have been involved in a TV Turn-Off, please write to me (see Author's Note on page 198), and add your Turn-Off to the list in future editions of *Unplugging the Plug-In Drug*.]

Notes

1. Urie Bronfenbrenner, "Who Cares for America's Children?" Address presented at the Conference of the National Association for the Education of Young Children, 1970.
2. Jim Trelease, *The Read-Aloud Handbook*. Penguin, 1985.
3. W. H. Dietz and S. L. Gortmaker, "Do We Fatten Our Children at the Television Set? Obesity and Television Viewing in Children and Adolescents." *Pediatrics* 75 (1985).
4. S. G. Burton, J. M. Calonico, and D. R. McSeveney, "Effects of Preschool Watching on First-Grade Children." *Journal of Communication* 29: 3 (1979).
5. D. W. Winnicott, *Mother and Child*. Basic Books, 1957.
6. Tom Valeo, "Television and Kids: Breaking the Habit." *The Daily Herald*, Arlington, Illinois, July 18, 1985.
7. Louise Jamieson, "With TV Set Off, Volume Goes Up as Families Talk." *The Riverdale Press*, December 26, 1985.
8. "Town Plans TV Turn-Off for Children." *Hartford Courant*, May 5, 1985.
9. From *S.E.T. Free*, the newsletter of the Society for the Eradication of Television, Albuquerque, New Mexico, July 1986.
10. Dottie Lamm, "Out the Window: Second Thoughts on TV." *Denver Post*, February 23, 1986.

Bibliography
Books and Articles Partly or Entirely about Television Use and Abuse or about TV Alternatives

For parents:

Elkind, David. *The Hurried Child*. Reading, Mass.: Addison-Wesley, 1981.

Goldson, Rose. *The Show and Tell Machine*. New York: The Dial Press, 1977.

Greenfield, Patricia Marks. *The Effects of Television, Videogames and Computers*. Cambridge, Mass.: Harvard University Press, 1984.

Honig, Alice Sterling. "Television and Young Children" in *Young Children* (May 1983).

Howe, Michael. *Television and Children*. Linnet Books, 1977.

Kaye, Evelyn. *The ACT Guide to Children's Television: How to Treat TV with T.L.C.* Boston, Mass.: Beacon Press, 1979.

Keeshan, Robert J. (Captain Kangaroo). "The Nurturing of Young Americans: Go Watch T.V." in *Vital Speeches* (May 15, 1983).

Lappe, Frances Moore. *What to Do After You Turn Off the TV*. New York: Ballantine Books, 1986.

Mander, Gerry. *Four Arguments for the Elimination of Television*. New York: William Morrow and Co., 1978.

Piers, Maria. *The Gift of Play*. New York: Walker and Co., 1980.

Postman, Neil. *Amusing Ourselves to Death*. New York: Viking, 1985.

Rogers, Fred. *Mister Rogers Talks to Parents*. New York: Berkley Books, 1983.

Singer, Dorothy and Jerome L., and Diane M. Zukerman. *Teaching Television—How to Use Your Child's Advantage*. New York: The Dial Press, 1981.

Trelease, Jim. *The Read-Aloud Handbook*. New York: Penguin Books, 1985.

Wilkins, Joan Anderson. *Breaking the TV Habit*. New York: Charles Scribner's Sons, 1982.

Winn, Marie. *Children Without Childhood*. New York: Penguin Books, 1985.

———. *The Plug-In Drug*. New York: Penguin Books, 1985.

For Children

Angell, Jodie. *First the Good News*. New York: Bradbury, 1983.

Berenstain, Stan and Jan. *The Berenstain Bears and Too Much TV*. New York: Random House, 1984.

Bond, Michael. *Paddington on Screen*. Boston, Mass.: Houghton Mifflin, 1982.

Brown, Marc, and Lorene Krasney Brown. *The Bionic Bunny Show*. New York: Atlantic Monthly Press, 1984.

Byars, Betsy. *The TV Kid*. New York: Viking, 1976.

Cohen, Miriam. *Jim Meets the Thing*. New York: Greenwillow, 1981.

Freeman, Don. *The Paper Party*. New York: Viking, 1974.

Heide, Florence P. *The Problem with Pulcifer*. Philadelphia: Lippincott, 1982.

Hicks, Clifford B. *Alvin Fernald, TV Anchorman*. New York: Holt, Rinehart and Winston, 1980.

Leroe, Ellen. *Confessions of a Teenage T.V. Addict*. New York: Lodestar Books, 1983.

Manes, Stephen. *The Boy Who Turned into a T.V. Set*. New York: Coward, McCann, and Geoghegan, 1979.

———. *The Oscar J. Noodleman Network: The Second Strange Thing That Happened to Oscar Noodleman*. New York: Dutton, 1983.

McPhail, David. *Fix-it*. New York: Dutton, 1984.

Phelan, Terry Wolfe. *The Week Mom Unplugged the TV's*. New York: Four Winds Press, 1979.

Lee, Polk, and Eda LeShan. *The Incredible Television Machine*. New York: Macmillan, 1977.

Shyer, Marlene. *Adorable Sunday*. New York: Charles Scribner's Sons, 1983.

Swarthout, Glendon. *TV Thompson*. New York: Doubleday, 1972.

Wright, Betty R. *The Day Our TV Broke Down*. Milwaukee, Wis.: Raintree, 1980.

Index